"I have known Jennifer for a number of yea... thorough, knowledgeable, and professional people I have worked with. *Claim Your SWAGGER* is a testament to these qualities."

—**Ben Chambers**
Head of Business School and Talent, People and Culture
Grant Thornton UK LLP

"For those raised in Western cultures, "swagger" can have a heavily laden male gender connotation, with images of the rugged American west and equally rugged cowboys coming to mind, so I was pleasantly surprised how Jennifer has taken the term and appropriately reappropriated it for the modern challenges of our post-pandemic world. *Claim Your Swagger* is an extremely accessible and enjoyable read with practical exercises and "go-dos" for the reader seeking greater personal growth and life balance. The book will take you on a deep and rewarding personal journey of discovery, often through the author's own heartfelt and transparent shared journey, through thought experiments, and case studies of others' genuine revelations and insights. I encourage you to discover how empowering it can be to claim your own SWAGGER through the gifts provided within these pages."

—**Tim Blakesly**
Assistant Dean, Executive Education
University of Southern California
Marshall School of Business

"In *Claim Your Swagger*, Jennifer gives us a fun, practical approach to discover and recognize the best (and worst) parts of yourself, and then do something positive with both. A spirited read!"

—**Peter Mulford**
Global Partner, Chief Innovation Officer
BTS

"The ultimate security in life is a strong sense of self-worth. When we know how our uniqueness makes a unique difference, we can truly live our purpose. In *Claim Your SWAGGER*, Jennifer Sukalo combines research and real-world experience to give you tools that can immediately help you thrive."

—Zach Mercurio, PhD
Author of *The Invisible Leader:*
Transform Your Life, Work, And Organization
with the Power of Authentic Purpose

"The word that comes to mind is WOW! Jennifer really takes readers on a journey to look into themselves and figure out what is important. She challenges you to leave the baggage at the door and focus on yourself! Jennifer truly makes you think about your past and who you are today because of the past. I am extremely excited to be working on my SWAGGER and cannot wait to see where this journey takes me!"

—Deb Jeffers
Executive Director
Central California and Hawaii/Guam
American Cancer Society

"This is not your grandfather's self-help book. Far from it. *Claim Your SWAGGER* is filled with common sense and actionable approaches for self-improvement."

—Craig R. Barrett
Retired CEO/Chairman
Intel Corporation

Claim Your SWAGGER

CLAIM YOUR SWAGGER

STOP SURVIVING AND START THRIVING

Jennifer Mrozek Sukalo

NEW YORK

LONDON • NASHVILLE • MELBOURNE • VANCOUVER

CLAIM YOUR **SWAGGER**

Stop Surviving and Start Thriving

Published in New York, New York, by Morgan James Publishing. Morgan James is a trademark of Morgan James, LLC. www.MorganJamesPublishing.com

SWAGGERU™ and P to the Power of 3 – Patience – Practice – Perseverance™ are trademarks of Ellowyn Group, LLC.

CliftonStrengths® and the CliftonStrengths 34 Themes of Talent are trademarks of Gallup, Inc. Gallup's content is Copyrighted by Gallup. Used with permission. All rights reserved.

The non-Gallup® information you are receiving has not been approved and is not sanctioned or endorsed by Gallup® in any way. Opinions, views, and interpretations of CliftonStrengths® are solely the beliefs of Jennifer Mrozek Sukalo, the author of this publication.

Proudly distributed by Ingram Publisher Services.

A FREE ebook edition is available for you or a friend with the purchase of this print book.

CLEARLY SIGN YOUR NAME ABOVE

Instructions to claim your free ebook edition:
1. Visit MorganJamesBOGO.com
2. Sign your name CLEARLY in the space above
3. Complete the form and submit a photo of this entire page
4. You or your friend can download the ebook to your preferred device

ISBN 9781636980669 paperback
ISBN 9781636980676 ebook
Library of Congress Control Number:
2022946109

Cover Design by:
Rachel Lopez
www.r2cdesign.com

Interior Design by:
Chris Treccani
www.3dogcreative.net

Morgan James is a proud partner of Habitat for Humanity Peninsula and Greater Williamsburg. Partners in building since 2006.

Get involved today! Visit: www.morgan-james-publishing.com/giving-back

To my sister Janine, who left this world far too early.

AUTHOR'S NOTE

The stories shared in this book are the author's recollection of events. Some of the names and identifying characteristics have been changed to protect the privacy of those depicted.

Any reference to definitions of words or terms is the author's recollection and a compilation of research from multiple sources.

IMPORTANT MESSAGE: This book is intended to provide useful information on the subject matter contained within. It is for informational and educational purposes only and is not intended and should not be used as a substitute for professional medical, psychological, financial, legal, or other advice, diagnosis, or treatment. The author is not diagnosing conditions or offering medical or mental health advice. The information in this book is NOT intended to be used for self-diagnosis or treatment. If you feel you require immediate help, please contact the appropriate authorities, medical providers, and/or crisis intervention service providers in your local area for immediate assistance.

~~ACKNOWLEDGMENTS~~
GRATITUDE

Gratitude is a large component of this book, so if you'll indulge me, I'd like to take this time to share my heartfelt gratitude for the many people who have supported, encouraged, challenged, dared, consoled, and lifted me up along this journey. I can't possibly name all of you in this short space, but just know that you have had a positive and profound impact on my life and for that, I'm eternally grateful.

I'm grateful for Elena Rover who introduced me to Constance Costas. Constance, you challenged me to find my voice and shift from professional writing to engaging with the reader in a more conversational tone. You also encouraged me to reach out to Morgan James. Thank you both.

I'm grateful for Annette Leal Mattern who has been a wealth of knowledge, guidance, and moral support even when life was knocking you down. Your spirit and perseverance have been an inspiration and blessing to me.

I'm grateful for David Hancock at Morgan James who firmly recommended that I send in my book proposal even when I didn't feel like it was ready. Thank you for pushing me outside my comfort zone and for believing in the book concept I shared with you. I'm grateful for Naomi,

Jim, Gayle, and the entire Morgan James team. You have become some of the best cheerleaders I have in my corner. Thank you all.

I'm grateful that I listened to my gut instinct when I was on the call with Rea Frey Holguin of Writeway™ and decided to enlist their editing services for my book. It's difficult to put into words how grateful I am for you, Joe Tower, editor extraordinaire. You have guided, emboldened, and nurtured me. You have commiserated and laughed with me. You have continued to foster the belief that I really am a writer, even when my belief faltered. Your willingness to share the rawness of your own struggles and how this book supported your journey is a priceless gift. Thank you, my friend.

I'm grateful for Marika Flatt, Emily Bond, and the entire PR By the Book team. Emily, your patience with me as I maneuver on the steep learning curve of social media has been nothing but miraculous. You have definitely earned several jewels in your crown. I'm certain this is the beginning of a long and beautiful relationship. Thank you.

I'm grateful for the leaders, cancer survivors, friends, and colleagues I've had the pleasure of engaging with over the years. Thank you for the stories, learning, and experiences you've provided which have helped shape the SWAGGER method.

I'm grateful for the words of wisdom and encouragement I received from Brené Brown, Robin Arzón, Jess Sims, Matt Wilpers, Steve Chandler, and many others. While I haven't had the opportunity to engage with you personally, your words were always there for me on the days I needed them most. You might not know it, but you have inspired me to keep going and face my fears head on. The only way is through. Thank you all.

I'm grateful for Kris Poole and Pam Thompson. Thank you both for your support and encouragement, and for challenging me to jump into the saddle even before I felt ready. The excellent care you've provided my horses has enabled me to focus on completing this monumental milestone. Thank you.

I'm grateful for my parents who instilled in me the idea that I could do anything I put my mind to. I'm grateful for my family and friends who have always been there for me. Thank you.

This list would not be complete if I didn't express how grateful I am for my husband, Peter. Your unwavering belief in me has kept me going. Your love, partnership, and friendship have kept me whole. You are my biggest fan and staunchest supporter. None of this would be possible without you. I love you beyond words and am so excited to be on this journey with you. Thank you.

TABLE OF CONTENTS

Author's Note   xi
~~Acknowledgments~~ Gratitude   xiii

Chapter 1   Who Stole Your SWAGGER?   1
Chapter 2   P to the Power of 3 – Patience – Practice – Perseverance™   11
Chapter 3   Discovering Your Self-Worth   31
Chapter 4   Gaining Appreciation for Your Strengths and Limitations   61
Chapter 5   Finding Gratitude for Your Life Experiences   95
Chapter 6   Becoming Grounded in Your Core Values   129
Chapter 7   Empowering Yourself to Overcome Self-Limiting Beliefs   161
Chapter 8   Being Renewed Through Your Passion and Purpose   197
Chapter 9   So, Now What?   231

About the Author   247
References   249

CHAPTER 1

Who Stole Your SWAGGER?

Picture a vibrant young woman at the top of her high school class. On the cheerleading squad, the student body council, and the homecoming court. She was outgoing and yet exceptionally good at keeping her own company. Don't get me wrong, she had lots of friends and acquaintances, but none that were what you might call "close." She had confidence and self-assurance that many didn't understand. Many people thought she was "stuck-up" or aloof, when, in fact, she was just fiercely independent.

This young woman had *swagger*.

She carried this confidence and independence with her into college, where she seemed to excel at everything. She taught fitness classes, placed third in her first bodybuilding show, and graduated cum laude. She loved standing out and being different and was known as the only cheerleader with short hair.

Now, she gave the impression that she had it all figured out, and that she didn't need anyone, and in the eyes of others, she was "Miss Goody-Two-Shoes," "Miss Perfect," someone who never did anything wrong. But notice those words here, "gave the impression," because we'll discuss it more later, and remember that the perception of others is often much different from reality.

Yes, I confess that this young woman was me. I paint this portrait because it's important for you to see and understand me so what follows has more meaning.

Now we're going to fast-forward a bit.

I got married at 23, a toxic and unhealthy relationship that lasted less than a year. By the time I turned 24, my husband and I were separated and beginning a lengthy divorce process. When the ink on the papers had dried, the divorce proceedings had officially lasted longer than the marriage itself.

By the end of the marriage, I was working three jobs and had ended up on the verge of homelessness, all my worldly possessions tucked away in a storage facility, under lock and key. You might be wondering why I didn't just move back in with my parents. They didn't live close enough for me to commute to any of my jobs. The only thing that kept me from living in my car was my aunt, who took me in.

I remember the day I hit rock bottom, distinctly. Laying crumpled on the family room floor of my aunt's house, hugging my knees to my chest, staring blankly out the sliding glass doors through tear-filled eyes—at the pool, the fenced-in backyard, the freshly cut grass.

The weight of it all had finally caught up with me.

At that time, I felt like Alice in Wonderland, with my world slowly, painfully shrinking around me, and the last thing I wanted to hear was dismissively exclaimed clichés like "this too shall pass," or "what doesn't kill you makes you stronger." Even though, deep down, I knew both to be true.

My current reality was, I had failed spectacularly. I had failed my family, my faith, but most importantly, myself. The once assertive, confident, positive young woman I had been had vanished. The person I saw in the mirror I barely recognized—an insecure, scared, utterly exhausted shell of a human being. I was lost. For the first time in my life, I had absolutely no idea how to move forward.

My swagger was gone, and I was sure that someone had stolen it.

You might be wondering what the heck I'm talking about, and what I mean when I say *swagger*? Well, let me explain. Have you ever encountered a person who simply "lit up a room"? There is just "something" about them that intrigues you and draws you in. They seem to exude an assuredness, a reserved self-confidence, a comfort in their own skin. They have an energy about them, almost as if they glow. It's an intangible quality you can't put your finger on, and if you were watching them dine at a restaurant, you would stop your waiter and let them know, "I'll have whatever they're having, please."

This . . . is *SWAGGER*, and, no, I'm not talking about your standard dictionary definition. I'm talking about the process of truly embracing who you are, stepping into the power you already have, and unleashing your untapped potential. And to do that, I've defined SWAGGER in a whole new way.

SWAGGER stands for:

SW Self-worth
A Appreciation for your strengths and limitations
G Gratitude for how your life experiences have helped shape who you are
G Grounded in your core values
E Empowered to overcome your self-limiting beliefs
R Renewed through a greater focus on your passion and purpose

I'm telling you about my SWAGGER because I want you to know that it wasn't stolen, I'd just never fully claimed it in the first place.

When you wholeheartedly claim your SWAGGER, you become unstoppable. You become that person who "lights up a room." The joy, happiness, and fulfillment you're able to create will seem unimaginable to those whose SWAGGER still eludes them. When you claim your SWAG-

GER, you bring the absolute best version of yourself to whatever you do, and when you're at your best, you perform at your best.

Claim Your SWAGGER is designed to help you claim—or in some cases, reclaim—what might feel like life has stolen from you. We've all survived something, whether it be abuse, assault, cancer, COVID-19, divorce, loss of a loved one, or some other trauma. In the wake of surviving these experiences, you might feel like you've lost particular pieces of yourself along the way, and that your SWAGGER, if you ever really had it, is gone for good.

But I promise you that your SWAGGER isn't gone, you just have to choose to claim it. You have to *choose* to move out of that place of despair and see that moment as the spark that creates the rest of your life, instead of something you merely survive. Your SWAGGER is never really gone; it just needs to be awakened with new fervor, with new intentionality and passion.

That's what this book is all about.

In the pages that follow, I am going to walk you through a method of embracing yourself, stepping into your power, and using what you already have to be who you were born to be, and at the end, you will reclaim your SWAGGER.

How do I know? Because I've not only lived it, I've also helped others do it.

Claim Your SWAGGER is the first of a three-book series. In it, I'm going to share with you the knowledge and expertise I've gained through my own SWAGGER journey and the numerous years I've spent working as a global leadership consultant. I'm going to give you access to my expertise that companies have paid hundreds of thousands of dollars for, and a program I've developed through work done with approximately fifty thousand leaders from around the world at various multinational and Fortune 500 companies.

All of that is now yours.

Claim Your SWAGGER will help you move from merely surviving your life to thriving in it. It'll guide you through each part of the SWAG-

GER method. You'll take exploratory steps to discover what makes you not only unique, but extraordinary, developing a new relationship with your self-worth. You'll gain an appreciation for your strengths as well as your limitations and find gratitude for how your life experiences have helped shape who you are today. You'll become grounded in your core values and learn to step into your power to overcome self-limiting beliefs that hold you back. Finally, you'll experience a sense of renewal through a greater focus on your passion and purpose.

Right now, I know that skeptical voice inside your head is muttering, "Yeah, right. Here we go again. What's this, the latest self-help craze?"

Well, I welcome that healthy skepticism and will offer a challenge in return.

"A challenge?" the skeptical voice is saying.

Yes, a challenge.

Let me show you what I mean.

I was delivering a workshop to a group of senior leaders in New York City. It was a single-day program with lots of material to cover. There was a gentleman there who we'll call Jeff, who kept questioning everything we were doing. Each time I turned around, Jeff had his hand in the air. "How's this supposed to work exactly?" he would ask. "Does this stuff actually work in the real world?"

Now, to be fair, Jeff was an attorney, so technically he was paid to be skeptical. However, I was trying to keep an entire room full of leaders engaged and moving through these activities, so I had to figure out a way to delicately approach Jeff without dismissing him or causing him to completely disengage from the session.

Here's what I said: "Jeff, I appreciate you asking questions and challenging the work. And so, I'd like to challenge you in return. My challenge for you is to suspend judgment. Come with us on the journey. If your questions aren't answered by the end of the day, I'll be happy to continue our discussion."

Well, you'll never guess what happened. As we convened to conclude the day, everyone was asked to share a "key learning" from the workshop.

When it was Jeff's turn, he stood up and said, humbly, "My key learning from today is to suspend judgment."

Okay, so this was one of those moments in life when I wish I could've just pressed the "pause" button. What a huge win! I wanted to jump up and down, throw my hands in the air, and scream "Yes!" In fact, I assure you, it was difficult to contain the utter delight I was feeling inside. Somehow, I managed to maintain my composure.

Like the challenge I extended to Jeff, my challenge for you is to suspend judgment and come along on this journey. You have nothing to lose, and you have all your SWAGGER to gain. Who knows? This could be the very best thing you do for yourself.

Of course, this will require courage and commitment on your part. But I'm not asking you to do the impossible. I am inviting you to embrace a challenge that is transformational and life changing. I've seen how this work has transformed people across the globe. You too can have this experience. If you are willing to do the work.

The first thing that I'm going to ask you to do is shift your mindset. This book technically falls under the category of "self-help," a term which I've never liked. Honestly? I hate it. Why can't we just call it "personal growth and development," our journey of continuous improvement? The term "self-help" gives the impression that we *need* help. To me, this isn't about *needing* help, it's about taking action and being productive, seeking to grow and develop, to always continuously improve.

Take an elite athlete, for example. How much time do they spend researching, honing, fine-tuning, reviewing past performances, just to shave a split second off their time or master a new subset of their skills? Athletes spend countless hours working on continuous improvement. Do we call their effort self-help? No, we do not.

So, you know what? We're not going to call our effort self-help either.

Now that I've gotten that off my chest, the more important question is this: how much time do you spend on continuous improvement or creating positive change? If you're anything like me, or the many I've worked with, you're often too caught up in *doing*—moving from one task to the next, solving problems, putting out fires, just to wake up and do it all over again the next day.

You can't simply read something and expect to see improvement or change. Creating change of any kind requires you to consistently do something different than you're doing today. It requires you to generate new habits and behaviors by forming new neural pathways. It requires you to take time to reflect, analyze, and learn from what you've done.

That voice in your head is likely saying, "Yes, but Jennifer, I don't have time for that." But the interesting thing is that we always seem to find time for what's important, our *priorities*. So where do you—capital Y-O-U, you—rank on your list of priorities? It's time for you to put yourself at the top of that list, instead of at the bottom. When you make yourself a priority, you'll figure out a way to carve out the time to get it done.

Now, let's tackle that trifecta of action items: *reflect*, *analyze*, and *learn*. A quote from a movie I watched some time ago has stuck with me: "Tell me, and I forget. Teach me, and I remember. Involve me, and I learn."

In *Claim Your SWAGGER*, you're going to learn through experience.

Think about some of the most powerful lessons you've learned. Chances are these lessons were ones that you learned through experience, from figuring things out on your own, not because of something someone told you. That's what experiential learning is all about—learning by experiencing—and it's without a doubt the most effective way.

Take, for example, a hot stove. The first time you burned your hand on a hot stove, you instantly learned never to do that in the future. Why? Because, when you think back to that experience, you remember that it hurt, and you don't want to feel that again. You recognize that it's only when the stove is hot that you need to avoid it. Your brain cataloged the information so that when you come across a hot stove in the future, you know not to touch it.

Claim Your SWAGGER utilizes an experiential learning approach, putting you at the heart of the process. The content and activities in the book are designed to help you *reflect* on your experiences, *analyze* what happened, and *make sense of* what you've *learned*. Ultimately, this helps you determine how you will *apply* that learning going forward. The goal is to help you develop new knowledge and skills that enable you to respond to situations differently and create lasting behavioral change.

Let me break things down a bit more.

Experience

There are multiple ways to experience things.

1. Experience through doing—our life experiences and situations we participate in (very powerful and sometimes very painful)
2. Experience through observation—learning from what others did, like through case studies and stories (way less stressful and painful)
3. Experience through experimentation/simulation—trial and error in a simulated environment, think of a flight simulator (you can crash without actually getting hurt)

Analyze

This is about reflecting on and breaking down the experience to uncover the learning.

1. What happened in that experience?
2. What was interesting or stood out for you in that experience?
3. What went well and what could have been done differently?

Rationalize

This is about making sense of what you've learned and identifying where and how you can benefit from the learning.

1. What learning can you take away from that experience?
2. What challenges or situations are you currently facing where the learning might be helpful?
3. Where else might the learning from this experience be helpful to you in your life?

Apply

This is about determining how and where you'll apply the learning, and what will be different as a result.

1. How will you apply the learning?
2. What specific steps will you take to apply the learning?
3. What will be different as a result of applying the learning?

Jack Nicklaus, arguably one of the best golfers of all time, talked about building golf courses during an interview, and specifically mentioned what he loves about creating new courses. He revealed that what excites him the most is unlocking the potential of each property he works on.

That's exactly how I feel about you. Yes, I'm talking to you. You have untapped potential just waiting to be unleashed. But, unlike Jack Nicklaus and his golf courses, I'm not doing the unlocking. You are. I will provide you the tools, the guidance, and the support so that you can liberate your potential, be the best version of yourself the world has ever seen, and claim your SWAGGER.

Still not sure?

Then I guess the most important question is this: are you happy with yourself and where your life is right now? I'm sorry to say, but I'm going to venture a guess that the answer is "no," or you wouldn't have picked up this book at all.

The next logical question is this: what are you waiting for? You're the only person who's going to turn your life around.

Life is so incredibly short. In the words of *New York Times* best-selling author and vice president as well as head instructor at Peloton, Robin Arzón, "Live your life. Do it now. This is not a dress rehearsal."

My sister Janine left this world far too early. She was just in her thirties. I always had the feeling that, for some reason, she wasn't able to figure out how to create joy and happiness in her life. It seemed like she was always trying to find external things to make her happy, by doing things for the wrong reasons and trying to please others. It's as if she was always looking for the next "when."

For example, "I'll be happy when I [graduate, get married, get promoted, have kids, etc.]."

What "when" are you chasing?

And guess what? It's not about "when." It's about "now." It's about finding joy and happiness in every moment. It's about being the best version of yourself. Not for someone else, but for you. Because when you're at your best, you've got so much more to offer and give to those you love, those you care about, and the world around you.

I can only wonder if I'd been able to help my sister see how amazing she already was, to discover what made her unique and extraordinary. I wonder if I could've helped her see that she didn't have to be more, that she just needed to be *her*, the person she was born to be. Perhaps she might still be here today.

I wasn't able to help my sister. But I am here for you now.

First, I'm here to tell you that you're not alone. You're a part of an amazing family that we call the human race. And now I welcome you to another family: an exclusive group of SWAGGER-seekers, like-minded individuals ready to step up and claim their SWAGGER as well. If you're ready to show the world how extraordinary you are, I'm here to guide and support you every step of the way.

Your time on this earth is short, so why not make the most of it? Why waste your precious time being stressed, unhappy, and unfulfilled? You already have everything you need. All you have to do is learn to use it.

Imagine you're a sprinter, up in the starting blocks, poised and ready. You don't have to wait for permission to get moving, though, because *you're* the one holding the starter's pistol. Just pull the trigger and run like your life depends on it—because it does. Your SWAGGER is waiting. Your future self is pleading. Do this for you right now.

Turn the page and start your SWAGGER journey.

CHAPTER 2

P to the Power of 3 – Patience – Practice – Perseverance™

Y ou did it! You turned the page! That's amazing! I'm thrilled that you've taken this step to begin your SWAGGER journey.

Now, for you to truly claim your SWAGGER and take advantage of all this book, and its corresponding content, has to offer, you'll need to dig deep within to find and engage in courageous self-exploration, relentless curiosity, and profound humility to be open and honest with yourself.

"Wait, what?" you're probably saying. "*Relentless* curiosity?!"

I know, it sounds hard and even a bit scary, doesn't it? Well, here's what I'm going to encourage you to do: lean into that feeling. Embrace it. That uneasiness means that you're about to do something outside your comfort zone, something worthwhile, something remarkable. You're about to embark on a journey that most people will never even dare to begin.

But remember, you're not like most people. You're a person seeking to claim your SWAGGER. That sets you apart from the rest.

Think of this self-discovery as your very own treasure hunt, and your SWAGGER is the treasure you'll claim. Yes, you're venturing into uncharted territory, but how exciting is that?! Just imagine what extraordinary discoveries await you along the way. The SWAGGER method serves as your map, and you'll unlock a new gem of that treasure at each stage of your journey.

So what can you do to guarantee your success?

Former US Secretary of State Colin Powell said this about success: "There are no secrets to success. It is the result of preparation, hard work, and learning from failure."

I couldn't agree more, but for our purposes, I like to put it in a slightly different way. Success requires a prescription that I call **P to the Power of 3 – Patience – Practice – Perseverance**.

To succeed on this SWAGGER journey, you'll need to adopt, apply, and embed this simple yet powerful formula. The good news is, once you learn the formula, it'll always serve you well in all aspects of your life—not just here.

Notice, I used the word "simple" above. I want to be honest with you here. Make no mistake, when I say "simple," that does not mean easy. While this formula is simple to understand and remember, that doesn't necessarily make it easy to do. Keep in mind, nothing worthwhile is ever easy. So let's get you prepped and ready for your journey by unpacking each element of this formula.

P to the Power of 3 – Patience – Practice – Perseverance

Let's begin with **patience**.

Patience is a virtue, so they say. Have you ever wondered who "they" are, and what that means exactly?

Well, I don't know if **patience** is a virtue or not. But I do know that the *Cambridge Dictionary* defines **patience** as "the capacity to endure what is difficult or disagreeable without complaining; the ability to wait for a long time without becoming annoyed or upset."

Not at all easy to do, in my opinion.

Given these definitions, I like to view **patience** as a choice. You have to choose whether to endure or to wait, and whether or not to complain or get annoyed or upset. If you're anything like me, this is a choice you have to make regularly because it's not something that comes naturally. In a world where you expect immediate responses and instant gratification, exercising **patience** is something of a lost art.

Take, for example, a sushi apprentice. Learning to master the skills required to expertly and traditionally prepare sushi takes an enormous amount of **patience**. Think about this: your ultimate goal is to become a sushi chef, and you're asked to spend the first three years of your training simply washing rice.

Once it's been determined that you've satisfactorily mastered washing rice, you might then be allowed to cook and prepare the sushi rice according to the special recipe used by the sushi master. You might spend the next two to five years cooking and preparing that rice. You're now five to eight years into your apprenticeship, and you've not yet once touched a single piece of fish. Would you have the **patience** to continue? I'm not sure I would.

This is a pretty extreme example. However, there are numerous situations you encounter daily where you have to make a choice—to wait, to endure, or not.

If you do *choose* to wait, then, how do you *behave* while you're waiting? Life provides wonderful examples if you stop and pay attention.

Let me show you what I mean.

I was recently in need of a new mobile phone. Mine was several years old and had decided to stop holding a charge after only a couple of hours. It was time. I'd been putting it off for a while. I think I needed to feel ready for the time, the energy, and, let's face it, the **patience** it was going to take. You have to go to the store, purchase the new phone, and then transfer everything over to the new device. It's a whole process. I know there are other ways to do it, but I like to get things done in one fell swoop. I'm not good at waiting around for a phone ordered online to arrive in the mail and then transferring all my data from the old phone over to the new phone all by myself, without help. No, that's just not a good idea.

So my old phone finally pushed me over the edge and let me know that the time had definitely come. The need outweighed the dread. There I found myself, standing in the store, waiting to be helped. Two couples were being helped ahead of me. I figured that it shouldn't take too much longer before it was my turn.

Oh, how wrong I was.

I waited. And I waited some more. And then even more. My initial instinct was saying, "Okay, this is taking way too long. I'm out of here." Instead, I took a deep breath and *chose* to be patient. "What makes me more important than anyone else?" I thought to myself. My rational brain chimed in as well. "Everyone here in this store has something they need help with."

I decided to challenge myself to pay attention to what was going on around me while I waited.

For one, there was a couple—let's call them "mature"—being assisted by one of the associates, who we'll call "Len." It looked like Len was helping them transfer data from an old flip phone to a new flip phone. To be honest, I didn't even know flip phones still existed. Whatever the case, the older technology wasn't communicating very well with the newer technology, so transferring the data was taking forever.

Now, I'm sure I know what you're thinking, so let me just say that, no, I was not *eavesdropping*. I wasn't close enough to hear everything that was being said in their conversation. And I wasn't being a voyeur. I was simply observing the overall interaction between Len and the mature couple. Okay? Good, I'm glad we could clear that up.

Len was exhibiting a calm demeanor. He was kind and supportive, like the nice tech support agent on the other end of the line who helps you navigate through the simplest of activities without making you feel like an idiot. He made that couple feel like they were the most important people in the room. They were all talking and laughing together. When Len realized that things were going to take much longer than he'd originally anticipated, he encouraged the couple to leave the phones with him so that he could take care of transferring the information without making them wait. The couple reluctantly agreed and said they would be back before the store closed to pick up their phones.

Finally, it was my turn, and I kid you not, when it was all said and done, I must've been waiting there at least 45 minutes.

But I walked up to the counter and I looked at Len and I said to him, "I am so impressed with the **patience** you exhibited while helping that couple. It was truly inspiring. I'm not sure I would've been able to keep my calm for that long."

Len was clearly surprised by my comment. "Thank you so much," he said. I think perhaps he was expecting me to berate him for taking so long. "I was simply trying to help," he continued. "I'm amazed that you noticed. So many people today are too self-absorbed to see what's going on around them."

At that moment, another employee, a gentleman who'd been cleaning up the store while I had been waiting, was getting ready to leave. Before he did, he said to Len, "Give her a super discount. She's waited forever and has been so patient." I smiled at him and thanked him as he left. Of course, what I was thinking was, *If he only knew how hard this was! How much effort it took for me to be patient!* As I mentioned earlier, **patience** isn't something that comes naturally—it's something I have to work at.

But, in that situation, that hard work paid huge dividends. Now I have a new phone that's working perfectly. And my new friend Len has asked that I keep him updated on the release date for this book because he can't wait to read it and share it with his wife. But more than any of that, I learned so much from that experience that will serve me going forward.

This experience reinforced to me the belief that **patience** is a choice. Again, you must *choose* to wait, *choose* to endure. Most importantly, you must choose how you *behave* while you wait. All of that is within your control.

So, how does that relate to you and your SWAGGER journey?

As you embark on this journey, you'll be asked to do new things. Difficult things that will stretch you and push you outside your comfort zone.

That means, however, that instead of being patient with others, you'll need to be patient with yourself.

Think about when you first learned to drive a car—if you drive, that is. You had to be intentional and focus on every step. You get in. You put your seatbelt on. You check the mirrors, put your foot on the brake. You turn the key or push the ignition. You put the car in gear.

After a long while, you probably started to make your drive to and from work, for example, without even thinking about it. Probably you wonder how you got between home and work at all because you don't even think about it, you know it all so well.

The act of driving, which was once a challenge, has now become second nature to you. Congratulations, you've created a habit. When you get in a car now, the neural pathways you've created in your brain move signals effortlessly without you having to use intentionality and focus. But to be clear, that took time. You didn't make this happen in a day, a week, or even a month.

Claiming your SWAGGER is a long-term commitment. It is going to take time to discover what makes you unique and extraordinary, and then to develop a new relationship with your self-worth. It is going to take time to gain an appreciation for your strengths and your limitations. It is going to take time to cultivate gratitude for your life experiences and how they've helped you become who you are today. It is going to take time to become grounded in your established core values and learn to step into your power to overcome "SWAGGER-limiting" beliefs that are holding you back. It is going to take time to create renewal through a greater focus on your passion and purpose.

But the first step to succeeding on your SWAGGER journey is **patience**. You need to recognize and appreciate that it's taken you a long time to become who you are today, and to create the habits—both good and bad—that govern your daily life. So you won't be able to simply flip a switch and expect to be a new you. Undoing old habits and creating new patterns of behavior is going to take time. Research from a 2009 study published in the *European Journal of Social Psychology* suggests that developing a new habit can take anywhere from 18 to 254 days, on average. That alone shows you why **patience** is such a critical part of this process. Therefore, you must be patient as you discover these new parts of yourself, as you try things on and see how they feel, as you begin to fully embrace who you were born to be. **Patience** will need to be a choice you make daily.

However, it's not enough just to be patient. That's only one piece of the puzzle. Forming new habits requires you to consistently execute new behaviors so you can strengthen the necessary neural pathways.

So, let's take a look at the second part of the **P to the Power of 3** formula.

Practice. You can't become good at anything you do without **practice**.

I'm sure you're familiar with the phrase "**practice** makes perfect." Well, I've always been fonder of the phrase "perfect **practice** makes perfect." The reasons for this I'll make clear in a later chapter, but whichever phrase you align with, the point is, **practice** is the key—the essential component without which you can't expect to become great, or even good, at anything.

I referred to the behaviors of elite athletes in the previous chapter. Well, now I want you to think about any elite performer: athletes, or even musicians or dancers. How much time do you think those performers spend practicing versus time they spend performing? Would you say 80 percent of their time is spent practicing to 20 percent spent performing? Seventy percent to 30 percent? Or would you say more like 90:10?

No matter which way you choose to calculate it, the reality is that these performers spend an enormous amount of time practicing their craft compared to the time they spend performing.

Typically, professional athletes **practice** anywhere between 5 and 6 hours a day, 6 days a week. Professional musicians **practice** 4 or more hours per day, also 6 days a week. Professional dancers **practice** up to 10 hours a day, 6 days a week. Now, yes, that's their full-time job, so you can assume they treat it as such, but any way you slice it, that's still a lot of time practicing.

Let's look at some other examples of what being committed to **practice** looks like. Two of my favorites come from movies.

In the film *Wild Hearts Can't Be Broken*, Gabrielle Anwar plays Sonora Webster, an orphan in the 1930s with a dream of becoming a "diving girl," one of the riders of the famous diving horses. Sonora is told that she's too young, too small, and not strong enough to be a diving girl. She's finally given a chance, but only if she can complete a moving mount. That means she has to perfectly time grabbing the harness and climbing on the horse's back as it gallops past her. Not an easy feat. Sonora **practices** and **practices**. She falls over and over again. She bloodies her nose, gets banged up, and gets bruised. But she keeps getting up. She keeps practicing and practicing until she finally achieves a moving mount successfully.

See, Sonora was fully committed to the **practice**. She wouldn't stop until she could do the new skill. She was willing to endure pain and discomfort. She was willing to overcome any challenge put in her way. Sonora wasn't letting anything get in the way of her accomplishing her dream of becoming a diving girl.

Another example comes from *Julie and Julia*, in which Meryl Streep plays the role of Julia Child, who decides she wants to attend the famous Le Cordon Bleu school to learn French cooking. Although Julia is the only woman in the class, she is undeterred and refuses to give up or be beaten.

There's a scene in the movie where the class is learning knife skills, specifically how to properly chop onions. Julia is very disappointed with her performance in class and decides to go home and **practice**. She buys countless onions and **practices** chopping and chopping until she has mastered her knife, and the skill. When her husband returns home that evening, he almost passes out from the onion fumes. But when Julia returns to class the next day, everyone, including the instructor, is impressed by her ability to quickly and effectively chop an onion.

Talk about commitment. If you've ever chopped onions, then you know that the onions can be murder on your eyes. But Julia wasn't going to let anything stand in the way of her success in, and graduation from,

Le Cordon Bleu, onion or no onion. She wasn't going to let any task, no matter how difficult, keep her from accomplishing her goal.

Both of these examples highlight the importance of committing to the **practice** of a new skill until it's mastered, no matter how challenging.

So, what about you? How much time do you spend practicing your moving mount or your knife skills? How many hours per day do you **practice** the sport you love? Or that musical instrument you're trying to learn? How much **practice** do you put into your job at work? How much time do you **practice** being a parent? What about leading your life—how much **practice** do you put into that? Because first and foremost, you're the elite performer of your own life. So how much time do you spend practicing becoming great, or even just good, at that?

If you're anything like me, or the thousands of leaders I've worked with over my years in corporate consulting, you probably spend most of your time "performing" your life, and not enough time "practicing" at it. So I guess the next question is: how good do you want to be at it? How exceptional do you want to be at leading your life?

I said that you can't become great or even good at anything without **practice**, and that's why it's the critical second step to succeeding on your SWAGGER journey. You have to be committed to practicing new behaviors until you've mastered them and they become your new habits. Now, I may not be asking you to **practice** for six hours a day six days a week like one of our elite performers. However, if you think about it, being the elite performer of your life *is* your real full-time job. What could possibly be more important than that? I'm asking you now to treat it as such and commit the time to the **practice** that is required for you to succeed.

To be clear, your **practice** involves more than just reading this book. Each chapter pertaining to a different component of the SWAGGER method contains activities and reinforcement exercises for daily development. These are designed to help you discover what you need to claim that part of your SWAGGER. Each activity has a suggested time allotment needed to complete it. This will assist you in identifying pockets of time in your schedule to set aside for your SWAGGER journey.

The suggested daily development provides opportunities to strengthen new behaviors associated with claiming your SWAGGER. These shorter and more frequent **practice** sessions reinforce the new behaviors and neural pathways you're working to create. The daily development suggestions can also be accessed through your computer or handheld device at swaggeru.com/my_swagger.

Now, I know this is all probably a little overwhelming, but here are some tips to help you succeed . . .

First and foremost, don't freak out. You've got this. Break your **practice** into smaller, bite-sized chunks to help make it easier to fit it into your already overscheduled day. It's as easy as blocking time in your calendar, just like you would for anything else: a workout, a doctor appointment, a lunch with friends, or picking your kids up from school. What gets scheduled gets done.

As I discussed in the last chapter, this is all about making yourself and your SWAGGER journey a priority in your life. Small steps lead to great success. You can identify and set aside these "windows" of time to get your SWAGGER **practice** in throughout your day. For instance, maybe you could take a quick break between Zoom meetings or calls. Or maybe there's a pocket of time on your commute to and from work. You even could fit in your SWAGGER **practice** instead of scrolling through social media feeds at the end of the day. Now, this will all require creating new routines, that's true, like waking up ten minutes earlier than usual and doing some **practice** before you get out of bed in the morning—you get the idea. Whatever the case, create a schedule that works for you. That means that you're in total control of the frequency and duration of these SWAGGER **practice** sessions, and my only ask is that you commit to doing some form of **practice** each and every day. That is critical to your success.

Ideally, it will be most effective if you can aim to build in three to five **practice** sessions per day. Remember, these **practice** sessions include all aspects of working on your SWAGGER journey, like reading subsequent chapters of the book, completing corresponding activities, reviewing corresponding affirmations, and studying the daily reinforcement suggestions.

So on a day when you have a bit more time, you might commit to reading a whole chapter, completing one of the activities for that chapter, and then doing one daily reinforcement suggestion for that chapter. On another day when your time is more limited, you might do three daily reinforcement suggestions spaced out at different times since those require shorter amounts of time. Again, you choose what works for you, but definitely aim to fit in three to five **practice** sessions per day.

Again, as another tip for success, do yourself the favor of physically booking time in your daily calendar for your **practice**.

"You mean you want me to, like, write it down in my calendar?" you're asking.

Yes, that's what I mean. Create meetings with yourself for this work. If you don't, you'll likely keep putting it at the bottom of your list and be distracted by other things that you will prioritize as more important at that moment. Remind yourself *why* you're doing this **practice**. When you claim your SWAGGER, you will bring the best of yourself to *everything* you do, so, I mean this sincerely, this self-development work will be the most important thing you can do if you'd like to give your best in all aspects of your life.

Alright, alright, I hear you, enough of the soapbox. I know you get it. Sometimes, though, I just can't help myself.

By now, I'm sure that you recognize the importance of both **patience** and **practice** as you embark on your SWAGGER journey. However, these two alone are still not enough. Remember that the formula is **P to the Power of 3**, not two.

The two movie examples I shared earlier about being committed to **practice** also highlighted another important facet of this work. They illustrated a willingness to endure discomfort, and sometimes even pain, in the relentless pursuit of a goal. Sonora and Julia didn't give up no matter how long it took or what challenges were in their way.

Let's explore why success will always elude you without this critical piece of the puzzle. This quality is called **perseverance**, and it's the third P in the **P to the Power of 3** formula.

Why do you think some of the most beloved stories in literature, television, and film often deal with someone overcoming adversity and finally succeeding in the end? It's because we get inspired by watching the strength of the human spirit in action. We see the characters in the story display determination and courage. For that brief time, then, you too believe that you can accomplish the unimaginable.

Well, guess what? You can with **perseverance**.

Perseverance is defined by Merriam-Webster as "a continued effort to do or achieve something regardless of difficulty, failure, or a delay in achieving success." So why is this, the third P in the **P to the Power of 3** formula, so essential for you to succeed on your SWAGGER journey? Simply, because in our human nature there is a tendency to give up when things get tough. Just like water always seeks its own level, your survival instincts often encourage you to seek the path of least resistance.

Think about it, when you use your GPS, you look for the fastest route, the most wide-open route, the route with the least traffic. When presented with route options, how often do you sign up for the one that's the most difficult? Right, exactly. But don't worry, there's no judgment here; that's just the way you're wired, and you're not alone.

Don't get me wrong, however, a lot of people love challenges, and in fact you might be one of them. You might embark with gusto on journeys to reach the lofty goals you set for yourself. But when things don't go as planned or become harder than expected, doesn't your enthusiasm wane? Your forward progress can slow to a crawl until you eventually quit. How many New Year's resolutions have you kept up for more than a couple weeks or even months after the first of the year?

Perseverance is what helps us overcome our natural tendency to give up—but where does it come from?

When I was training for my only bodybuilding show, my coach used to ask me, "How badly do you want it?" Now, if you saw me today, it'd be evident that this took place eons ago because, these days, I look nothing like a bodybuilder. Of course, I hesitate to even tell you this because there are so many more dramatic stories of **perseverance** out there, some of which I'll share later. But it does demonstrate that **perseverance** is essential, not just for heroes in the movies, but for everyday people like you and me.

In my case, I had to want success in competitive bodybuilding badly enough that I was willing to put in the training time and bear the pain that comes with transforming the body. I had to be fully invested and ready to endure training sessions that brought me to tears and made me sick, to push through and complete that last repetition even when every cell in my body was telling me that I couldn't.

I had to want it badly enough to reshape my entire life to focus on my training. I had to be willing to train—logging in mile after mile of more cardio and hour after hour of training—while my friends were out on Saturday nights. I had to believe that every drop of sweat would be worth it. I had to want it badly enough that I was willing to completely change my diet and give up all the things I adored eating. I can still remember going out to dinner with my family and watching them all drink margaritas and eat à la carte tacos, while I sat there with a plate of plain chicken and steamed vegetables. I would ask if I could just smell their food just so I could pretend I was eating it. Actually, my mouth is literally watering right now as I write this. It was agonizing, and so much more than just the physical pain of working out and building muscle.

Listen, though, this is not about you feeling sorry for me. I did that to myself. I chose to go down that path. Crazy, I know. I share it with you to help you see where **perseverance** comes from. It comes from desire. You have to want the thing you're working for more than you fear it. Your desire to achieve your goal has to outweigh your fear of any discomfort and pain that might stand in your way.

When it comes to this pain and discomfort, of course, bodybuilders aren't alone. Marathoners and other endurance athletes know all this too well. You have to possess incredible amounts of **perseverance** to complete 26.2 miles, 50 miles, 100 miles, or an Iron Man Triathlon (I know, and here you thought I was crazy). These amazing athletes are completely out of their minds. Their desire to achieve their goals, to reach those finish lines, far outweighs any suffering they will surely experience along the way.

This is **perseverance** in spades.

One of my favorite displays I've ever seen of **perseverance** in sports came recently, during the 2022 Australian Open. It was an incredible match between 35-year-old Rafael Nadal and 25-year-old Daniil Medvedev. Trust me, you don't have to be a tennis fan to be in awe of what transpired.

Nadal was down two sets to love (i.e., 0), and his win looked hopeless. However, one of the things I appreciate most about Rafael Nadal is that he never gives up. He never believes he has lost until the last ball is struck. Well, he proceeded to win the next three sets and claim his 21st Grand Slam title. It took almost five-and-a-half hours for him to accomplish this goal, but he didn't let anything stand in his way. Can you even imagine how tired he must have been, or how hard it had to be to stay focused for that long without giving in?

It's almost impossible to come back from two sets down in a professional tennis final—well, I guess not impossible, since Nadal did it, but highly improbable. Most people would've felt discouraged being down two sets in a final. The statistics weren't in his favor. But he didn't let this deter him. He just kept playing, one point at a time and one set at a time, until he achieved victory.

It is truly inspiring and amazing to watch **perseverance** in action.

Athletes aren't the only people who display **perseverance**, of course. In my work with cancer survivors, I was constantly humbled by not only the strength and determination, but the **perseverance** these remarkable people exhibited. No matter how exhausted and weak they felt from treatment, no matter how many surgeries they endured, no matter how many times the cancer came back, they never gave in or gave up. They were singularly focused on their goal: to not only beat cancer, but to not let it beat them.

Take, for example, Amanda. She's an ovarian and breast cancer survivor. She's been battling this relentless disease for decades and has been through numerous surgeries and treatment protocols over the years. Yet, no matter what she's been asked to endure, Amanda has never lost her spirit or her fight. This battle of hers is one that will last for the remainder of her days because, in her unique situation, cancer is always lurking around the corner, just waiting to emerge somewhere else in her body. However, you wouldn't know any of this if you spoke with her. Amanda is so full of life and steadfast and resolute in her refusal to allow cancer to define her or to win. Her daily display of **perseverance** is extraordinary.

There are many stories of war veterans who've demonstrated **perseverance** both on and off the battlefield. The story of Carl Brashear is one such story, highlighted by the movie *Men of Honor*. Brashear, famously portrayed by Cuba Gooding Jr. in the movie, overcomes poverty, lack of education, racism, and hatred to become a United States Navy deep-sea diver. During a salvage diving exercise, an accident on deck severely damaged Brashear's left leg. Rather than accept the medical retirement the Navy suggested, he chose to have his leg amputated and worked tirelessly to be reinstated to full diving duty.

In the movie, there is a famous scene depicting Brashear's reinstatement hearing, where he is faced with yet another challenge: to walk twelve steps while wearing a new deep-sea diving suit, which weighed over 200 pounds. The Navy didn't believe that Brashear's prosthetic leg would support the weight of the suit. Master Chief Sunday, played by Robert De Niro, helps Brashear suit up and begins counting his steps. When it seems Brashear cannot continue, Master Chief Sunday screams at him. "Cookie, I want my twelve!" he shouts. This emboldens Brashear, and he stands up straighter. More determined than ever, he takes one excruciating step at a time until he completes all twelve and is reinstated to full diving duty.

Brashear didn't let anyone, or anything, stand in his way. He was the first African American amputee to undertake Navy diving duty. Two years later, he earned the rank of Master Chief and continued to dive for another nine years before finally retiring.

If Carl Brashear isn't well known to you, what about Walt Disney? Or Oprah Winfrey perhaps? Both those household names persevered through unimaginable circumstances to become the icons we know so well today. They never gave up, no matter how dire their situations became.

Oprah grew up in poverty and suffered through years of sexual abuse, which began when she was only nine years old. She got into trouble with the law and was on a path to destruction. Did she give up? No. Against all odds, she figured out a way to continue her education, finish her studies, and start a career in broadcasting. Oprah now runs a media empire and is one of the wealthiest entertainers in the world.

Walt Disney was fired from his newspaper job as a young man for lack of creativity. He was on the brink of starvation when his animation company failed. He was even told that his signature character, Mickey Mouse, would never succeed. But he kept moving forward. He didn't let setbacks, rejections, or failures keep him from making his dream a reality and giving birth to the magical world of Disney we know today.

The list goes on and on. Yes, some of these individuals are famous, and you probably can't even imagine what the world would be like if they'd given up. But guess what? They're no different from you. They accomplished extraordinary things because they persevered. They refused to let anything stand in the way of accomplishing their goals and realizing their dreams.

So, all that's left now is to ask yourself, "How badly do I want it?" How badly do you want to claim your SWAGGER? You have to want it more than you fear it. Your desire to be unstoppable, to be that person who lights up the room, to create unimaginable joy, happiness, and fulfillment in your life, has to be stronger than any challenge you'll face along the way. Even when those challenges come from unlikely places. Believe it or not, some of the challenges you'll face will come from within you—the voices inside your head, which we'll discuss in Chapter 7. Additionally, some challenges will also come from people who are supposedly your "friends."

There's a strange dynamic in the world. There are people in your life who claim to care about you and yet the minute you start to change, to improve, they become naysayers instead of encouragers. They become haters. Why is that? It's because those people are afraid of your success. They want you to stay the same, to be unfulfilled, just like them. Triathlete, public speaker, and author David Goggins says it this way: "We live in a world with a lot of insecure, jealous people. Failure terrifies them. So does our success." If you start to step into your power, to become the person you were born to be, there are those around you who will become less relevant, and that will scare them.

So, what does this mean for you? It means you need to start seeking out people who'll support you, challenge you, and encourage you on this journey. Don't worry too much, you'll start to recognize pretty quickly the people in your life who're excited by your success, versus those who want to drag you down. So, prepare yourself to weed out the naysayers and the haters. On this journey, you will have no time for toxic people where you're headed.

Okay, that's a lot of information, so let's recap:

To succeed on your SWAGGER journey, you need to apply the **P to the Power of 3 – Patience – Practice – Perseverance** formula to every aspect of your journey. **Patience** both with the journey and with yourself. **Practice**, or the commitment necessary to execute new behaviors to develop new habits. **Perseverance** to endure the challenges that will lay ahead. Furthermore, you also need to create a support structure by surrounding yourself with those individuals who'll hold you accountable and encourage you.

If we were to plug these components into the form of a mathematical equation, your success would look something like this:

$$(\textbf{\textit{Patience}} \times \textbf{\textit{Practice}} \times \textbf{\textit{Perseverance}}) + \textit{Support} = \textit{Success}$$

To make this official, to hold both you and I accountable for the journey you're undertaking, I am going to ask you to craft and sign a formal **commitment statement.**

You can use the template below, or you can also go ahead and craft one using your own words. Handwrite or type it out. Then, print it and sign it.

THE SWAGGER JOURNEY COMMITMENT STATEMENT

- *I commit to choosing **patience** daily. I recognize that claiming my SWAGGER takes time.*

- *I commit to making time to **practice** daily, to strengthen and reinforce new behaviors.*

- *I commit to having **perseverance**, to staying the course no matter how long it takes or how difficult it becomes.*

Signed _____

Date _____

Place your signed **commitment statement** somewhere you'll see it every day, first thing: by your bed, on your bathroom mirror, or above your coffee maker. Speak aloud the commitment statement every morning when you wake up and each night before you go to bed. Try to make this action part of your new daily routine. Commit to yourself daily to have **patience**, to make time to **practice**, and to have **perseverance**, regardless of what you encounter on your journey.

To demonstrate the strength of your commitment, you can feel free to share your **commitment statement** with the rest of the SWAGGERU community at swaggeru.com/my_swagger.

When you share your **commitment statement** with others, it helps to make the journey itself, and your decision to embark on it, real. It can be easy to give up on yourself, and it's much harder to quit something that you've shared publicly. Once you've shared your commitment with the SWAGGERU community, it's no longer a commitment that only *you* know about.

Now, do yourself another favor: say "yes." Say yes to your commitment to your SWAGGER journey. The treasure hunt for self-worth begins now.

Turn the page to find out what the first part of the SWAGGER method has in store for you.

 ## SWAGGER Insight

- Success requires **P to the Power of 3 – Patience – Practice – Perseverance.**
- **Patience** is the ability "to endure what's challenging or unpleasant, or to wait for a long time without complaining, becoming irritated, or upset."
- **Patience** isn't a virtue, it's a choice that must be made regularly. You must choose to wait and endure and choose how you behave during the process.
- Claiming your SWAGGER is a long-term commitment. It's taken you a long time to become who you are today, and to create the habits—both good and bad—that govern your daily life.
- Developing new habits can take anywhere from 18 to 254 days.
- Perfect **practice** makes perfect.
- You can't become great, or even good, at anything without **practice.**
- You must be committed to practicing new behaviors until you've mastered them and they become your new habits.
- Make yourself a priority and physically schedule time in your calendar to **practice.**
- Break your **practice** up into smaller, bite-sized chunks.
- Aim for three to five **practice** sessions per day.
- **Perseverance** is "a continued effort to do or achieve something, regardless of difficulty, failure, or a delay in achieving success."
- It's human nature to seek the path of least resistance. Claiming your SWAGGER requires **perseverance** to overcome the tendency to give up when things get tough.

- You have to want it more than you fear it.
- Your desire to be unstoppable, and to create unimaginable joy, happiness, and fulfillment in your life, has to be stronger than any difficulty or challenge you'll face along the way.
- People are afraid of your success and will try to sabotage your efforts.
- Seek out people who challenge, support, and encourage you.
- *(Patience × Practice × Perseverance) + Support = Success*

CHAPTER 3

Discovering Your Self-Worth

I f someone you loved asked you why you loved them, what would you say?

For example, what if your child asked you to explain *why* you loved them? Would you tell them, "It's because of how attractive, smart, and funny you are?" Would you say it's because of the kind of job they have or how much money they've earned? Or what about because of how good they are at a particular sport or how many friends they have?

I am willing to bet that you wouldn't tell them any of these reasons. In fact, I bet you'd likely tell them it's because of *who* they are—period, full stop. You would tell them that just being who they are is enough, that there are no other conditions required to be worthy of your love.

So now let's turn that same question toward *you*. What about you? What makes you worthy of another's love? More importantly, what makes you worthy of your own love? The answer, really, should be the same as above. Because *you* are worthy of love just the way you are, just by being you, no other conditions required.

But, unfortunately, if you're anything like the numerous people I've worked with over the years, you don't believe this. My question to you, then, is *why*? Do you have any ideas? Is it possible to answer that question?

31

If not, don't worry. In this chapter, you're going to discover the current state of your self-worth, explore what might be keeping you from feeling worthy of love from yourself and others, and take steps to develop a new relationship with your self-worth.

The Current State of Your Self-Worth

Before you explore the reasons why you might not feel worthy, it's helpful to assess the current state of your self-worth.

Now, you might be thinking, "Well, wait a minute, Jennifer. Shouldn't you define self-worth before you ask me to assess it?" That's a good point, and for now, for these purposes, let's use your current understanding of what self-worth is as you come along with me on this journey of assessment and see what new ideas you discover about it. I promise you, as you move further into the chapter, more will be revealed.

Below is a brief assessment questionnaire. Answer the questions as honestly and openly as possible, but don't overthink it. Remember, there are no "wrong" answers, only "your" answers. The more honest and open you are with yourself, the more helpful the information you obtain will be.

Circle the number that corresponds to your response to each statement. When you've finished, add the numbers you've circled together to create a total. There are ten statements, so if you circled the number 5 corresponding to "strongly agree" for all of the statements, then your overall total would be 50.

Please note, this isn't a scientifically validated instrument. It's an assessment that's been designed specifically to help you gain perspective on your own self-worth today.

When you're ready, take a moment to complete it and tally your total:

Self-Worth Assessment

	Strongly Disagree	Disagree	Neutral	Agree	Strongly Agree
I feel better about myself when I think I look attractive.	1	2	3	4	5
The opinions other people have of me impact how I feel about myself.	1	2	3	4	5
I feel good about myself when I perform better than others.	1	2	3	4	5
When other people are proud of me, it makes me feel better about myself.	1	2	3	4	5
I like myself better when other people think I look attractive.	1	2	3	4	5
Having lots of people that care about me makes me feel worthwhile.	1	2	3	4	5
I feel better about myself when I'm doing well at work.	1	2	3	4	5
How other people see me has an impact on how I see myself.	1	2	3	4	5
Crossing things off my list helps me feel worthwhile.	1	2	3	4	5
When other people dislike me, it makes me feel worse about myself.	1	2	3	4	5

Okay, great. That wasn't so hard, was it? Now, I'll get to what your total means in a little bit because I'm sure you're anxious to see how things measure up. Recall that we just talked about **patience** in the last chapter, so it's time to employ that now. Before we get to totals, I'd like to ask you a few questions:

1. What main themes can you identify from the statements in this assessment?
2. How do these themes relate to one another?
3. What impact do these themes have on your self-worth?

There are three main themes that are contained in the statements of this assessment. One theme has to do with how you look, or how attractive you are to yourself and others. Another theme deals with the opinions of others toward you, whether they like you, care about you, or are proud of you. The third theme revolves around performance, like completing tasks, performance at work, and measuring your performance against others.

If you identified any one of these three themes, then you are getting it. Good for you. If you identified all three, you are spot on.

I'm sure at first glance these themes might not necessarily seem related. However, if you look closer, you'll see that all three of these themes are related to *external* factors. What do I mean by external factors? Well, external factors refer to things that influence you from the outside. So, in this case, the themes in these statements deal with your *outward* appearance, the opinions of *others*, and your *physical* performance. All of these are external factors.

Now, to the issue of impact: what do you think might happen if you allow external factors to influence your self-worth? (I know it's infuriating when I answer a question with another question, but it's something I will do quite often in this book because it will help you think more deeply, so just humor me here.)

So, any ideas?

That's right.

When you allow external factors to influence your self-worth, you open your self-worth up to volatility. Why is that? Because of the inherent nature of external forces. "External" means that these are factors that you are not in control of. So if you open yourself up to letting your self-worth be influenced by factors that aren't within your control, it is going to put your self-worth in a very vulnerable state.

Now let's talk about the total you came up with from your assessment and what it means for your self-worth.

Similar to golf, the lower your total is on this assessment, the better. A lower total score on the assessment signifies a stronger sense of self-worth. A higher total on the assessment, however, indicates a greater opportunity for strengthening your self-worth. Take a look at the following ranges to see where you fall:

- **10-20** You have a strong sense of self-worth that external factors don't significantly impact.
- **21-30** Your sense of self-worth shows promise, but there's room for improvement.
- **31-50** Your sense of self-worth is at high risk from external factors and would benefit from additional strengthening and development.

There's something very important I want you to understand, though, which is that no matter where your self-worth ranks right now on this scale, this is a journey to claim your SWAGGER, and your focus is on continuous improvement.

Think back to the previous chapter, when we talked about **P to the Power of 3 – Patience – Practice – Perseverance**. Remember that daily practice is critical for your success. This includes practicing behaviors that reinforce and strengthen your self-worth. If your self-worth is neglected, it could weaken over time and become vulnerable to the external forces you're bombarded with every day.

Connecting the Dots

By now you've hopefully started to formulate some ideas about why you might not feel worthy of love from yourself or others. One of the main culprits is that you've lost sight of your true self. You've spent your life connecting who you are to external factors, such as what you do or what you have. So let's see what happens when we follow the logic. If you're worthy just by being who you are, but that's dependent upon external factors, then, by default, your worthiness is also connected to those external factors.

Here's an exercise: what happens if you take those external factors away? Well, for starters, you don't know who you are anymore. If you don't know who you are, then you certainly aren't going to feel worthy of love from yourself or anyone else. You have come to believe that you're only worthy because of what you do or have, and if you take that away, then you're no longer worthy. Something that was once unconditional, then, you've now placed conditions on.

See how that works? Now, I know from experience exactly what this feels like. I'll never forget when a therapist said to me once, "I still haven't found any reasons to hate you, so why do you?"

At the time, my marriage was falling apart, I was working three jobs to make ends meet, and I was an emotional wreck. Luckily, the company I was working for offered therapy as part of the benefits plan.

That therapist hit the nail on the head. It was only when I'd taken time to reflect on what she said that it started to become clear. The voice in my head had been repeating this mantra: "I'm an achiever. I accomplish things. I don't fail." Then, I started to realize that I'd connected my self-worth to accomplishments and achievements my entire life.

The problem was, at that moment, I *was* failing. So many things in my life weren't going according to plan, so where did that leave my self-worth? You can pretty much tell by what the therapist said to me that my self-worth had taken a huge blow. The only thing I had to determine was whether this was a fatal blow or one I could recover from.

Let me give you another example.

Amberley Snyder is a professional barrel racer, author, and public speaker. In 2010 she suffered a life-altering injury in a car accident that left her paralyzed from the waist down. In the film *Walk. Ride. Rodeo.*, which documents her life, there's a scene that illustrates this point beautifully. Amberly is speaking with one of her friends, who suggests that she think about doing something other than barrel racing and rodeo. To this Amberley says, "It's not just what I do, it's who I am."

See, Amberley's entire sense of self revolved around her ability to compete at the highest levels in her sport. Initially, due to her accident, that was taken away from her, so what she had always used to measure her worthiness was suddenly gone.

So, now what?

I'm sure this might hit pretty close to home for you—except for the barrel racing part, of course. But let me ask you a question. How do you typically introduce yourself to others when you meet them? I'm guessing that it probably sounds a little like this: "Hi my name is [fill in the blank], and I'm a [doctor, teacher, chef, construction worker, parent of three beautiful kids, etc.]."

You might be saying right now, "So what's wrong with this, Jennifer? Doesn't everyone introduce themselves this way?" To that, I'd say, "Yes." You'd be correct in your thinking there. Most people in our modern society do introduce themselves in this same manner. That's because, even from a young age, we've all been *taught* to connect who we are with something outside ourselves—external factors.

When you were a kid, how did you introduce yourself? You introduced yourself by stating your name and then probably how old you were. But at a certain age, that falls away, and that's when you begin to tout your accomplishments. You might share things like what school you go to, what position you play in sports, or what scholarship you received. Finally, when you reach adulthood, the focus is on your job. If you really think about it, you've spent your entire life connecting *who you are* to *what you do*.

The problem with that is this: who you are is comprised of much more than just what you do.

So what does any of this have to do with your self-worth?

Let's take a look at how self-worth is defined. Self-worth is considered the belief that you have innate worth, that you're lovable and valuable as a human being irrespective of your traits, qualities, or abilities. Let's take a look at one word in particular: "innate." That word, used in this context, means that your worth is "inborn; natural." It means that you're worthy, not because of what you accomplish, how you look, or how good you are at the things you do. You're worthy simply because *you are*. You were *born worthy*.

Let all that sink in for a second before we move on.

Okay, now that we've clearly defined "self-worth," a good delineation to make right now is how that "self-worth" differs from our "self-confidence" or "self-esteem."

While often used interchangeably, self-esteem and self-confidence aren't the same as self-worth. Self-confidence is considered the trust and confidence you have in your abilities, qualities, and judgment, while self-esteem is known as a perception of self that ranges from positive to negative and revolves around how you view your traits, qualities, and abilities.

And the single greatest difference between all three of these terms relates back to that one word: "innate." Self-worth is the belief that you have worth irrespective of traits, qualities, or abilities.

See the difference?

Yes, self-worth is strongly connected to your self-confidence and self-esteem. If your self-worth is strong, then you'll likely have high self-confidence and self-esteem. The opposite is also true. If your self-worth is not strong, chances are that your self-esteem and self-confidence will be weak as well.

The Secret They Don't Want You to Know

Think back to the assessment you took earlier. There were three themes running through the statements in the assessment, one of which focused on the opinions of others, or how other people see you, remember? Another reason you might not feel worthy is because you've allowed others to tell you what you're worth, to determine the measures that you must meet to be worthy of love. If that's true, you've authorized others to be your judge and jury, while you sit like a defendant in the courtroom, waiting to hear the verdict—will you be worthy or not?

This "trial" began at an early age. First, you looked to your parents and those who raised you to help formulate how you'd measure your self-worth. As you move through life, the judge and jury change, as well as the power they hold, shaped by life experiences (something you'll explore more in Chapter 5). Through these life experiences, you've learned to adapt and adjust to win favor with whoever the judge and jury currently are, and you've become adept at determining what you need to do to be deemed "worthy" by your court.

The coronavirus pandemic has given new meaning to the phrase "wear a mask." But the truth is that you've been wearing masks since long before the pandemic started. These masks can't be seen by the human eye, but they're there. These are the masks you put on to show your judge and jury that you're smart, successful, happy, courageous, confident, or whatever other qualities you believe will help you plead your case for worthiness. Just take a look on Facebook, Instagram, or other social media outlets. What do you see? One mask after another, bolstering feelings of self-worth chasing likes and followers, constantly checking back in with the judge and jury to see whether they're buying your plea. Will you be found worthy?

You use these masks to protect yourself—from being judged, from being found guilty of not living up to the expectations you believe have been placed on you, and from being "executed" from worthiness. You believe that just being you, your authentic self, isn't enough. You're afraid that the judge and jury won't find you attractive enough, accomplished enough, or successful enough to be found worthy. You're afraid that you won't measure up to the exacting standards of the media-crazed and false-perfect world your judge and jury preside over. "What if they see the truth?" you tell yourself. "What if they see that I'm just me?"

There are countless stories about people pretending to be someone else—not even to succeed, but just to fit in. They're afraid to show who they truly are because it might change the perception others have of them.

In the movie *My Week with Marilyn*, there's a scene where Marilyn Monroe, played by Michelle Williams, encounters a group of fans while she's supposed to be out enjoying a day off in the countryside. She turns to her companion and asks, "Should I be her?" She then "transforms" herself into what her adoring fans, as well as the rest of the world at that point, expected her to be. She didn't feel free to be herself, she had to continually portray the "blonde bombshell," the existence of which she attributed to her blessings, and ultimately was her curse. Marilyn only felt worthy when she was loved and admired by the world.

There's a wonderful book starring Grover from Sesame Street that takes a slightly different look at this same situation. In *The Monster at the End of This Book*, Grover is so afraid of you, the reader, turning the pages because there is a monster at the end. But it turns out that it is Grover, all along. He is the "monster" at the end of the book. So, why is he so afraid of being seen? Because he is afraid to show you his true self. He is afraid that you might think of him as a "monster," and that he wouldn't measure up and be deemed worthy.

Speaking of readers: what about you? Are you afraid of showing the world who you truly are? Are you afraid that your judge and jury will see you as a "monster" at the end of the book? I urge you to recall the definition of self-worth. It's the belief that your worth is innate, that you are worthy simply because you exist. This means that *nothing* and *no one* can determine your worth but you. The judge and jury have power because you gave it to them, and now it's time to be courageous and take it back.

Lean in close. This is the secret that they don't want you to know. I define 'they' as the judge and jury, and anyone else whose opinion you care about. Are you ready? When you stop caring what these people think of you, then you release the power they have over you. That's absolutely worth repeating.

When you stop caring what these people think of you, then you release the power they have over you.

That's how you take your power back. They don't want you to know this because they like having power over you. They delight in the ability to manipulate you, to have you hang on their every word, hoping they like your post, or positively comment on your Twitter feed.

I know you might be thinking, "How do I just stop caring what other people think?" Well, it's scary for sure. However, when you finally manage to do it, you'll feel so liberated and wonder why in the world you didn't do it sooner.

Did you ever have a run-in with those mean girls or boys when you were going to school? Now, I'm going to date myself a bit, but here it goes. Back before they had cyberbullying, people used other methods to bully, shame, and hurt those they disliked.

I was on the receiving end of that bullying and harassment. I used to get crank phone calls from these two girls in school. Yes, this was on the home phone, which was a landline, not a cell phone. I know, right? I would answer the phone, and they would play these awful songs that were basically suggesting that I was a dog, I was trash, and I was worthless.

You see, I'd made the cheerleading squad along with one of the two mean girls. However, her best friend didn't make the squad. Now, I don't know why they singled me out to bully and harass, but they did.

I remember getting really upset at first. And then suddenly, I realized that I had a choice. I could choose to let them upset me or not. It was my choice, not theirs. This was a huge revelation.

I thought about why they were mad at me, which still didn't make any sense, but once I figured out that it was their issue and not mine, I was able to let it go. I was determined not to put any energy into what they were doing, not to let them win. I decided to act as if nothing had happened.

Guess what? It worked brilliantly. They continued for a bit but then lost interest. I think it was because I didn't give them what they wanted. I didn't let them have power over me. I didn't allow them the satisfaction of hurting me.

You can imagine how difficult this was at such an impressionable time in my life. We'd only just moved to the area the year before, so I was still the "new kid on the block," relatively speaking. Making friends and being liked were important to me.

However, instead of focusing outward for approval, I focused my attention inward. This quiet inner strength that had always been there for me is what helped me get through this experience. It was as if, even at that young age, my self-worth was telling me that those people had no right to dictate my worth, that I was worthy regardless of what other people thought.

This was a powerful lesson that has stayed with me and served me well. It's especially poignant now, given the fact that I'm getting ready to put this work out into the world for all to see. That's where courage comes in.

Courage isn't the absence of fear, but the willingness to do what you're afraid of. Well, I'm definitely afraid. This is one of the scariest things I've ever done in my life. Oh, there will be haters. There always are. Those individuals who are just waiting to pounce and attack.

But I can't worry about them. I know the secret, and that means I have a choice. I can stand up and say to the judge and jury, "This is me! Take me or leave me. I know I'm not for everyone and that's okay. I'm doing it anyway."

Best-selling author, researcher, and storyteller Brené Brown says that "courage starts with showing up and letting ourselves be seen." So, how about it? Are you ready to show the world the truth, your true self? If I can do it, so can you!

You know the secret they don't want you to know. So, make your choice. Choose not to care and watch their power fade away. All that's left is to muster up as much courage as possible and just go for it. You can do this! You're ready.

Making the Shift

Okay, so, let's get to it! It's time to start developing a new relationship with that self-worth by decoupling "who you are" from "what you do" or "what you have." It's time to take back the power you gave away to the judge and jury long ago and walk out of that courtroom for good, because, my friend, you are free.

I know you're probably thinking, "Wait a minute, Jennifer. That all sounds good and seems simple, but how exactly do I do that?" Don't panic. We'll get to it.

If you recall from the last chapter, just because something seems simple, it doesn't make it easy. Like all aspects of claiming your SWAGGER, developing a new relationship with your self-worth will take **P to the Power of 3 – Patience – Practice – Perseverance**.

You're going to continue to develop and strengthen your self-worth as you move through your SWAGGER journey. The more you learn about who you are and what makes you unique and extraordinary, the stronger your sense of self-worth will become.

Let's explore how you can start building your self-worth and reclaiming what's innately yours.

Changing Your Mindset

One of the most powerful steps you can take in developing a new relationship with your self-worth involves creating a mindset shift.

What do I mean by mindset?

Well, a mindset is considered a set of beliefs, attitudes, or assumptions that shape how you interpret and respond to situations. The experiences you have throughout your life shape the mindsets you hold. Your mindsets encompass things such as how you see yourself, how you view and engage with others, and how you perceive your circumstances and the world around you.

For example, if you've lived your life with the mindset that your glass is always half full, then you consistently work to see the upside of situations. On the contrary, if you've lived with the mindset that the glass is always half empty, then you tend to see the negative aspects of situations and perhaps struggle to find the positive. The mindset you hold influences how you respond to and interpret situations.

I was in New York City a while back, getting ready to facilitate a workshop for a group of leaders at a financial institution. My husband and I used to live there, so I of course know how loud and noisy the city can be. I was in my hotel room, settling in for the night, and I put my earplugs in as I was getting ready for bed. When I'm facilitating, I often get up incredibly early to prepare for the day, which requires me to go to bed quite early. In this particular situation, that meant that I was going to bed well before "The City That Never Sleeps."

It was unusually noisy that particular night. My hotel room must've been on a lower floor, and opened out onto the street, because even with earplugs, I couldn't believe how loud it was. I was struggling to get to sleep. I found myself complaining about the noise. "Don't they know that I have to get up early tomorrow? Don't they care about anyone but themselves? How's anyone supposed to get any sleep around here?"

But then, suddenly, I stopped whining, and I asked myself one very simple question. "Shouldn't I be grateful that I can hear?"

Boom.

The shift that question created was profound and immediate. I went from complaining to appreciating. This experience helped shape a new mindset that I now live by. Instead of looking at the glass as half full or half empty, I focus on being thankful that I have a glass at all.

This is what I mean by mindset shift. When you're able to adjust your mindset, you can create powerful and profound changes to the way you are responding to the world around you. Sometimes the shift can take place instantaneously, as it did for me. However, some shifts might require a significant amount of time to take hold.

It might be too great a leap to ask you to immediately shift your mindset right now, as if flipping a switch to turn something "off" that's been switched "on" inside you for such a long time. It might be too difficult to automatically adopt the belief that your worth is innate, irrespective of your talents, traits, or abilities. We'll let that take place over time as you continue on your SWAGGER journey. But let's begin by focusing first on creating some mindset shifts around who you are—your authentic self.

The Privilege of Being "You"

The first shift I'd like you to consider is introducing the idea that being your true self is a privilege and not a burden. Carl Gustav Jung, a psychiatrist and psychotherapist who's considered the founder of analytical psychology, said it well: "The privilege of a lifetime is to become who you truly are."

Take a look at the word "privilege." I realize that word has gotten something of a bad reputation of late. However, to clarify, I'm not talking about "entitlement." What do you think the difference is? It's all about perspective. Entitlement suggests something is owed to you, something that is your right, God-given or otherwise. On the other hand, privilege suggests something that's unexpected, almost like a gift that you're grateful to have. See that difference? When you're entitled, you have a sense of expectation, whereas, with privilege, there's a sense of gratitude.

We'll talk a lot more about gratitude in Chapter 5, but for the purposes of this context, I ask that you see privilege as the following:

- An opportunity to do something special or enjoyable—"I've had the **privilege** of working to help people create positive and sustainable change in their lives."
- A special advantage possessed by a particular person or group—"Don't regret getting older, it's a **privilege** denied to many."

When you look at something as a privilege, your entire attitude shifts and you see things from a completely different perspective.

Let me show you what I mean.

In my first year of college at California State University, Fresno, I got a job as a fitness instructor at a local gym. I couldn't believe my luck. I thought this was the best job in the world. I was getting paid to do what I'd do on my own anyway.

Now, this was way before the days of Peloton, The Mirror, Tonal, etc. (I know I'm dating myself again), back in the days when people went to the gym and took in-person classes. I know a lot of people still do this, but to get the right visual for the story, think back to the days when "aerobics" was all the rage. There's no need to go as far back as Jane Fonda, for goodness' sake, but you get the idea.

This gym was one of the largest in the area, and the "GroupX Room," as it was called, was about the size of a basketball court, but cut in half lengthwise. The room was situated so that the front and back of the room were the widest parts of the rectangle, the walls were covered with floor-to-ceiling mirrors, and there was a large, raised platform in the front of the room to make it easier to see the instructor.

Classes were consistently packed with exercise-addicted people like me who craved challenging, high-energy classes. I earned quite a few nicknames (and terms of endearment) as an instructor. "Cruella de Vil" and "Psycho Instructor from [*bleep!*]"—you fill in the blank—are two that really stood out (people also used to ask what my "caff-o-meter" was, because, apparently, they could gauge how intense the class was going to be by how much caffeine I'd ingested so far that day).

One afternoon, as I gathered my things to get ready to leave after class, a woman we'll call Mary came up to me. Because I used to sweat a lot, and still do, I'd wear visors to keep the sweat and hair off my face when I taught classes. Sweat soaked and with tears in her eyes, she handed me a visor that she and her daughter had decorated and personalized for me.

"I can't thank you enough," she said. "I've accomplished so much since I started taking your classes. I've lost weight. My strength and energy have improved significantly, and I finally feel like I'm able to be the person and mom I want to be."

"Mary," I said, "you're the one who's done the work. You made this happen, not me."

To that, Mary replied, "No, you don't understand. Because you were here, I was here. I was able to accomplish these changes in my life because of you."

This was one of those pivotal moments in my life. It was as if a blindfold had been taken off and I could finally see. Mary had opened my eyes and helped me recognize that teaching these fitness classes was so much bigger than me. It wasn't about getting paid to exercise, as I had originally thought. It was about being able to positively impact every single person in that room.

My mindset completely shifted. I no longer saw it as a job, but as a privilege. From that moment on, every time I stepped onto that platform, I knew it was another opportunity to be an inspiring presence, and to help the people in the room create profound change in their lives.

I named that new mindset I had formed, calling it "The Privilege of the Platform." I've carried it with me since that very moment and use it in all aspects of my life. The platform might not be teaching fitness to a room full of people anymore, but the concept stays the same. Every interaction is a privilege, an opportunity to positively impact people around me. This is what I mean by the word privilege. What I once thought of as a job had transformed into a priceless gift to be cherished and treasured.

Now it's time to create a mindset shift of your own.

One of the ways you can take back your power and start to build your self-worth is by seeing that being your true self is a privilege instead of a burden. Think of your authentic self the same as your fingerprint. Just as your fingerprint is unique to you, no other human being on this planet can be your true self. It also means that no one else can tell you how to be your authentic self. No one else can tell you who to be. Only you have that power. See it as the gift it is. Stop fearing it and start embracing it. Be bold enough to show the world who you truly are, your extraordinary self. Stop letting other people try to tell you who to be.

Just like in the song "Broken & Beautiful" sung by Kelly Clarkson, you've got this. You're enough, and you're phenomenal. You don't need anyone else to tell you who to be. You just have to keep reminding yourself that it's a privilege to be you, and no one can take that away from you unless you let them. You have to remind yourself that it's your uniqueness that makes you extraordinary. Stop trying to be like everyone else. Embrace who you are. Learn to use what you already have and unleash your potential. Be who you were born to be.

You might be thinking, "Jennifer, you make it sound so easy, but I don't know how," but just remember this: a mindset shift starts with shifting your thoughts. You're in control of your thoughts, they don't control you (we'll talk a lot more about this in Chapter 7). For now, if you want to shift your mindset, you have to be aware of your existing "old" thoughts so you can stop them in their tracks, then replace them with your improved "new" way of thinking. What you're doing is creating new neural pathways.

Think of it like this: your thoughts are a high-speed train, and to arrive at a new destination, you have to shift the train onto a new set of tracks. You're the one in the control room and you have to ensure that the train successfully shifts to those new tracks, otherwise you're not going to be able to pull the train into that new station. The key point here is that *you're* in control. You're the one who flips the switch. Pretty exciting, isn't it?

Let's revisit the half full or half empty glass metaphor we discussed earlier. In that noisy hotel room in New York, my thoughts were only focused on complaining—on the negative, already headed in the wrong direction. The first step toward the mindset shift was awareness—noticing where my thoughts were headed. The second step was to stop and shift. I did this by asking a new and different question: "Shouldn't I be grateful that I can hear?" That question stopped my thoughts from continuing down the negative track and shifted them onto a different and more positive track, which helped me arrive at a much healthier destination.

You have the power to do the same thing. Just like in my example, the first step is awareness of your current thoughts. For instance, let's say that perhaps you just came in fifth place in a competition. Your thoughts automatically start to travel in a direction of negative self-talk. "You loser," you say. "How could you come in fifth? Aren't you supposed to be good at this?" The more you let those thoughts run, the worse you feel about yourself.

The second step is to stop and shift. You have to stop those current negative thoughts right in their tracks and shift them in a positive direction. You can do that by asking a new and different question. In the situation of placing fifth in a competition, and immediately reacting with negative self-talk, ask yourself, "Is this something I believe? Or is this my judge and jury putting my self-worth on trial again?" Or instead of asking disparaging questions, ask productive ones. You could ask things like, "What did I do well? How could I build on that to improve in my next competition?"

You get the idea. Don't worry, I'll provide more suggestions in the daily reinforcement recommendations at the end of this chapter.

You Are Dynamic

Let's take a look at another mindset shift that will help you take back your power and build your self-worth. This shift revolves around the idea that who you are, your authentic self, isn't static. Instead, it's agile and dynamic.

Think back to the example I shared about barrel racer Amberley Snyder. Her sense of self was static. Initially, it was solely based on her ability to compete in barrel racing and rodeo. Following her accident, she had to create a new sense of self. While Amberley did eventually figure out a way to compete again, she also recognized that she was much more than merely her ability. She found satisfaction in the opportunities she had discovered to positively impact and inspire others by sharing her story and being a living example.

In the ever-changing world we all live in, your sense of self, how you view and measure yourself, has to be able to change and evolve. If it's static, like Amberley's, when the one thing you've related it to no longer exists, you're going to be left lost and vulnerable. Perhaps you've always measured your worth by your ability to do your job, to be the best in your sport, or to be an exceptional parent. But what happens when those circumstances change and how you normally measure yourself is no longer there? You will lose sight of yourself and begin to doubt your worth.

Let me shed some more light on this.

During a leadership workshop I was delivering in Malaysia to a group of senior leaders from a global pharmaceutical company, I met Amaresh. There were hundreds of people from over thirteen countries represented at this session, from all over Asia and the Middle East, and Amaresh approached me on a humid evening as we gathered outside for a cocktail reception just before dinner.

I was standing under one of the outdoor ceiling fans contemplating how anyone could remotely think it's a good idea to hold cocktail receptions and dinners outside in excessively humid climates (I'm very fond of air conditioning), so I'm sure I was trying not to look like I was melting when Amaresh came up to me seeking advice.

"I'm the head of one of the manufacturing plants," he told me. "I've always focused on being number one in all that I do. The problem is that my plant is quite small in comparison to many of the other plants in the company." He continued, "There's no way for me to be number one, as the other plants will always come out ahead of me."

Once he finished, I simply said, "Find your number one somewhere else." Amaresh looked at me, puzzled at first, so I shared some additional thoughts.

"You don't have to give up on being number one. You just need to tap into what makes you unique and extraordinary to be number one in another way. You could be number one in retaining top talent. You could be number one in growing other leaders and careers. You could be number one in employee satisfaction or quality."

Suddenly his eyes lit up as he realized the countless opportunities he could now explore. "That's brilliant," he exclaimed, with a smile from ear to ear. He thanked me and walked away with renewed excitement. You could just see the wheels turning in his head as he thought about which idea he was going to try first.

Like Amberley, Amaresh needed to expand his thinking around how he measured himself. He had a very narrow perspective on what "number one" meant to him. When his circumstances changed and his view of number one was out of reach, he lost a benchmark and an ability to measure his worth and value. Once he broadened that viewpoint and adopted an agile and dynamic mindset, he began to see that there were numerous ways he could add value, which significantly improved his sense of self-worth.

You might feel similar to Amberley and Amaresh, that it feels good to be productive, or to feel like you've accomplished something. After all, one of the three themes in that self-worth assessment was centered around performance. However, maybe it's time to broaden your perspective on how you measure your performance or accomplishments.

Instead of just focusing on being the best, or checking everything off your list, or completing a successful project, start asking yourself some new questions. How did you add value today? How did you have a positive impact on someone else today? How did you use something that you're good at to help someone today? Asking different questions will help you adopt a dynamic mindset around measuring your sense of self. You'll discover new ways to add value and improve how you see your worth.

Now, you'll need to reinforce these mindset shifts as you continue on your SWAGGER journey. The judge and jury won't be happy when you stop giving them the power they're used to holding, which means you'll need to stand strong and keep strengthening these mindset shifts through daily practice. Remember, the **P to the Power of 3 – Patience – Practice – Perseverance** formula applies to every step of the SWAGGER method.

You'll succeed if you're **patient** with yourself, do your **practice**, and keep **persevering** no matter how easy it might be to fall back into your old patterns.

I've said it before, and I'll say it again. You've got this. We're just taking it one step at a time. The best way to get something done is to simply begin, so, how about it? Are you ready to get started? If so, let's take a look at some activities and daily reinforcement suggestions to support your efforts. For additional activities and daily reinforcement suggestions, you can visit swaggeru.com/my_swagger.

Activity: Identifying Your Greatest Opportunities
Time: 15 minutes

Now that you've gained additional clarity around your self-worth and some of the factors impacting it, I'd like you to redo the self-assessment. This time, focus on identifying where you have the greatest opportunities to improve your self-worth. Use this as a tool to guide your practice and ensure that you're getting the most out of it.

For example, perhaps you had higher totals for the statements relating to the opinions of other people, and lower totals for the statements revolving around performance. This means that your greatest opportunity for improvement lies in practice that will bolster your self-confidence and self-esteem so you can minimize the power and impact that other people's opinions have on your self-worth. See how that works?

Step 1
Answer the questions below honestly and openly by circling the number that corresponds to your response to each statement. Don't overthink it. There are no "wrong" answers, only "your" answers.

The more honest you are with yourself, the more helpful the information you obtain will be.

		Strongly Disagree	Disagree	Neutral	Agree	Strongly Agree
1	I feel better about myself when I think I look attractive.	1	2	3	4	5
2	The opinions other people have of me impact how I feel about myself.	1	2	3	4	5
3	I feel good about myself when I perform better than others.	1	2	3	4	5
4	When other people are proud of me, it makes me feel better about myself.	1	2	3	4	5
5	I like myself better when other people think I look attractive.	1	2	3	4	5
6	Having lots of people that care about me makes me feel worthwhile.	1	2	3	4	5
7	I feel better about myself when I'm doing well at work.	1	2	3	4	5
8	How other people see me has an impact on how I see myself.	1	2	3	4	5
9	Crossing things off my list helps me feel worthwhile.	1	2	3	4	5
10	When other people dislike me, it makes me feel worse about myself.	1	2	3	4	5

Step 2

Add the numbers you've circled together to create your total. There are ten statements, so, if you circled the number 5 corresponding to "strongly agree" for all of them, your total would be 50. A lower total signifies a stronger sense of self-worth. A higher total indicates a greater opportunity for strengthening your self-worth. Take a look at the following ranges to see where you fall.

- **10-20** You have a strong sense of self-worth that external factors don't significantly impact.
- **21-30** Your sense of self-worth shows promise, however, there's room for improvement.
- **31-50** Your sense of self-worth is at risk from external factors and would benefit from additional strengthening and development.

Step 3

Look at the numbers to the left of each statement. Record the numbers for the statements where you answered "agree" or "strongly agree." In the example below, you would jot down number 1.

		Strongly Disagree	Disagree	Neutral	Agree	Strongly Agree
1	I feel better about myself when I think I look attractive.	1	2	3	4	5

- Statements 1, 5, and 8 have to do with how you look or how attractive you are to yourself and others.
- Statements 2, 4, 6, and 10 deal with the opinions of others toward you, whether they like you, are proud of you, or care about you.
- Statements 3, 7, and 9 are focused on performance, completing tasks, performing at work, and measuring your performance against others.

Based on the numbers you recorded, identify the theme or themes that represent your greatest opportunity for improvement. Then, go to swaggeru.com/my_swagger to find activities and daily reinforcement suggestions related to the specific theme or themes that affected you the most.

Activity: A.O.K.
Time: Varies

A.O.K. stands for **acts of kindness**. This is one of my all-time favorite activities. Before I get into the steps, let me first ask you a question: how do you feel when you've been able to help someone else? It feels great, doesn't it?

A fast and simple way to strengthen self-esteem is to help someone else. You might remember that your self-worth is strongly connected to your self-esteem, and of course, your self-confidence. Focusing on and strengthening your self-esteem will have a positive impact on your self-worth. The bonus with this activity is that you're putting kindness out into the world.

Step 1
When you wake up in the morning, set a target number for how many **acts of kindness** you will aim to accomplish that day. Remember that the more you do, the better you will feel. Also, keep in mind that you want to set yourself up for success, so make sure that your target is realistic.

Step 2
Acts of kindness no matter how small can be incredibly powerful. Below is a list of some suggestions, just to get your creative juices flowing. There are opportunities to perform acts of kindness in all aspects of your daily life. Keep your eyes open and pay close attention to the world around you for inspiration.
- Holding the door for someone.
- Helping someone carry something awkward or heavy.

- Giving up your seat to someone on the bus, train, etc.
- Telling someone they have a beautiful smile.
- Thanking someone for their service.
- Paying for someone's coffee or meal behind you in line.
- Leaving someone an extra tip to say thank you.

Step 3

Keep a record of the **acts of kindness** you perform and note how they make you feel. You have no idea the impact your kindness will have on someone else. You could be the bright spot in their day or the difference they needed.

Back in New York City, I was at the bar ordering drinks while waiting for a table at a restaurant. The bar was slammed. There was no room to move at all, and the bartenders were working their tails off trying to keep things moving.

There was a person to my right who clearly thought he was the most important person in the room, and he just laid into one of the bartenders, yelling at him for not finishing his order before starting on another. It was not a pleasant scene to behold.

When that not-so-pleasant individual finally left, I leaned over the bar and thanked the bartender. "I've noticed how hard you're working to keep things moving and ensure that no one waits too long for their drinks. I truly appreciate you and your service. Thank you."

Toward the end of our dinner, the bartender came over to our table and brought us a cheese course to finish our meal.

He said, "I just wanted to thank you so much for what you said to me earlier. You have no idea how close I came to quitting my job at that moment. Thank you for acknowledging me and my service."

Daily Reinforcement: Notice, Stop, & Shift
Time: 5 minutes

Step 1
Find a quiet place to sit down. Close your eyes and listen to your breath. On the inhale, say quietly to yourself, "Inhale." On the exhale, say quietly to yourself, "Exhale." Do this for one minute to clear and calm your mind.

Step 2
Think of a time when your thoughts ran away with you in a negative direction. Perhaps you made a big mistake, someone called your idea impractical, or you failed at something. Capture what you said to yourself at that moment.

Step 3
Record some questions you could ask yourself that you could use to shift your thoughts to a more positive track when faced with a situation like that in the future. Below are some suggestions to get you started.

- Is this something I believe or what someone else believes?
- What facts do I have to back up this thinking?
- What did I learn from this experience that will help me in the future?
- What did I do well and how do I keep doing more of that?
- What am I grateful for right now?

Daily Reinforcement: Affirmations
Time: 3–5 minutes

Affirmations are short positive statements designed to help reprogram your thinking, challenge negativity, and solidify your new mindset shifts. There are three keys to creating success with affirmations.

1. Write statements that resonate with you. These statements need to be meaningful for you. You won't have success with affirmations that mean something to someone else.
2. Set all your affirmations in the present. Your statements need to be anchored in "I am" not "I will be."
3. Say them with conviction. You have to say the statements with feeling and belief. If you're skeptical when saying your affirmations, your mind won't believe you.

Step 1

Craft a list of affirmations related to who you are and your self-worth. Below is a list to get you started.

- I am exceptional.
- I am worthy just the way I am.
- I am enough.
- It's a privilege to be who I am.
- I have everything I need.

Step 2

Print out your list of affirmations and place them by your bed. Say your affirmations first thing in the morning when you wake up and right before you go to sleep at night.

SWAGGER Insight

- When you allow external factors to influence your self-worth, you open your self-worth up to volatility because those external factors aren't within your control.
- You've spent your life connecting *who you are* to *what you do*.
- Who you are is comprised of much more than just what you do.
- Self-worth is the belief that you have innate worth, that you're lovable and valuable as a human being, irrespective of your traits, qualities, or abilities.
- You're worthy, not because of what you accomplish, how you look, or how good you are at the things you do. You're worthy simply because *you are*. You were *born worthy*.
- Self-esteem and self-confidence aren't the same as self-worth.
- Self-confidence is the trust and confidence you have in your abilities, qualities, and judgment.
- Self-esteem is a perception of self that ranges from positive to negative and revolves around how you view your traits, qualities, and abilities.
- Self-worth is strongly connected to your self-confidence and self-esteem.
- When you allow others to determine your worth, you've authorized them to be your judge and jury, while you sit like a defendant in the courtroom, waiting to hear whether you'll be deemed worthy or not.
- You wear masks out of fear that you're not enough, that your judge and jury will find you guilty of not living up to their exacting standards.
- The secret they don't want you to know is that when you stop caring what these other people think of you, then you release the power they have over you. They don't want you to know this because they like having power over you.
- Courage isn't the absence of fear but the willingness to do what

you're afraid of.

- Shifting your mindset is one of the most powerful steps you can take in developing a new relationship with your self-worth. You have to decouple "who you are" from "what you do" or "what you have."
- A mindset is a set of beliefs, attitudes, or assumptions that shapes how you interpret and respond to situations.
- Your life experiences shape the mindsets you hold.
- When you shift your mindset, you can create powerful and profound changes in the way you respond to the world around you.
- Being your true self is a privilege and not a burden.
- When you see something as a privilege, your entire attitude shifts and you see things from a completely different perspective.
- Who you are, your authentic self, isn't static; instead, it's agile and dynamic.
- Developing your self-worth requires **P to the Power of 3 – Patience – Practice – Perseverance.**

CHAPTER 4

Gaining Appreciation for Your Strengths and Limitations

I
f you could have a superpower, what would it be? X-ray vision, the ability to fly, superhuman strength?

Now, what if I told you that you already have superpowers? You do. You have SWAGGER superpowers. While these powers won't give you the ability to lift cars or shoot fire from your fingertips, they can help you claim your SWAGGER when you learn how to use them effectively.

Intrigued? Good, you should be.

Before we dig into your SWAGGER superpowers, I'd like you to complete the following activity.

Read through the statements below and check the ones that resonate most with you:

☐ I always write a to-do list.

☐ I always write a to-do list, even on the weekends.

☐ I always figure out the plot of a movie well before the end.

☐ I always sort my clothes according to color.

☐ I always ask lots of questions.

- ☐ I always find someone to race against, whether driving, cycling, running, etc.
- ☐ I always press the elevator button just to remind it that I am still waiting.
- ☐ I always remain skeptical unless provided with proof.
- ☐ I always challenge myself to complete tasks.
- ☐ I always find a way to create structure in my day and love to follow the same routine.
- ☐ I value meaningful conversations in small groups.
- ☐ I am that person who strikes up a conversation no matter where I am.
- ☐ I have a small circle of close friends.

When I used this in a corporate workshop, I would ask leaders to stand up for each statement that felt like them. It was like playing a big game of Whack-a-Mole, with people standing and sitting and standing and sitting as I read off each statement. But there was always an immediate and abrupt response when someone connected with a statement, and they'd stand up like they'd been shot out of a cannon.

Similar to all those many leaders in my workshop, if you were to do this activity with a friend, say, chances are they would stand for slightly different statements than you would. You probably didn't have to think much about each statement either, simply saying to yourself, "Yup, that sounds like me," and checking the box. Or you laughed at one of the statements, wondering, "Who does that?" and moved on to the next. To your friends, family, and coworkers, some of the statements you chose might seem quite quirky, but to you, that's just how you are.

I, for one, always have a to-do list. I've even been known to finish something and then write it on my list, just so I can check it off. My husband, however, takes his to-do lists to the extreme. The lists he makes just for the weekends, for example, are what many people wouldn't set out to accomplish in a week or a month, and he gets really upset when he can't complete them.

So you're probably asking, "Okay, Jennifer, so what does all this mean?" Well, these unique and somewhat peculiar things about you—these statements you've selected as particularly resonating with you—are the clues to your SWAGGER superpowers.

How?

Let me explain.

A New Way of Thinking

See, your SWAGGER superpowers develop from your *strengths*. So, to better understand your superpowers, you first have to discover your strengths and where they come from.

To begin that exploration, we must first turn to Don Clifton.

Don Clifton is regarded as the father of "strengths psychology." He studied the performance of individuals across various professions and industries. What he found paved the way for a theory about what individuals' inherent strengths are and how they develop as performers. He found that the best performers in any role are those who intentionally and consistently play to their strengths and are well aware of their limitations.

How is this different from other approaches?

This new way of thinking suggests that peak productivity can be gained simply by managing your weaknesses and focusing on your strengths. I know, it seems crazy, and completely opposite from what we're used to, but why is it so hard for us to wrap our heads around this concept?

Well, I've got a question for you. If you received a report card with all **As** and one **F**, which grade are you *naturally* going to focus on? Exactly. Your natural tendency is going to be to take a look at that big fat **F** and ask yourself, "So what the heck happened here?"

However, this unorthodox approach to personal development would have you focus on what you're good at instead of the shortcomings. This goes against your natural tendencies and how you've been conditioned to respond for years. Using a strengths-based approach suggests that you alternatively focus on the **As** and ask yourself, "So what the heck happened *here*?" It encourages you to identify what you did well to get the

As, and figure out how you can apply whatever that was to the area that caused you trouble and earned you an **F**.

See the difference?

For years you've been influenced to look at all your faults, highlight your performance gaps, and work to improve them. Strengths-based development turns this old way of thinking on its head, its foundational concept is centered around the idea that "fixing" weaknesses might indeed prevent future failure, sure, but it certainly won't "create" success. Success, this approach posits, is only achieved by focusing on and developing your strengths, while being aware of and managing your weaknesses.

So what does it look like, you might be wondering, to focus on your strengths and manage your weaknesses?

Here's an example: in the movie *The Greatest Showman*, actress Rebecca Ferguson plays an opera singer named Jenny Lind. Now, in approaching the role, Ferguson knew that her strength would be in the acting, not, obviously, singing, and no matter how much practice she put in before the cameras started to roll, she'd never be able to pull off an onstage performance as an opera singer.

So she enlisted the help of singer Loren Allred, a performer whose strengths are firmly in her ability to sing. The two partnered up to bring to life one of the most amazing songs from the movie soundtrack. Allred recorded the song herself, and Fergusson acted it so well that one might not even realize she hadn't actually sung a word without looking it up.

This is merely a shallow illustration of the power that you hold when you intentionally stay focused on what you're good at. Ferguson managed her weakness, focused on her strength, and had the presence of mind to enlist the help of another to complement her.

To recap, all your SWAGGER superpowers develop from your strengths, and since I'm also a Gallup Certified Strengths Coach, I'm here to help you discover yours.

The next step in discovering and homing in on your strengths is to gain a better understanding of where they come from.

Your Innate Power of Potential

Just like your favorite band might have a greatest hits album, you were also born with greatest hits—your *talents*.

Talents are the way you inherently think, feel, and behave. They come naturally to you and are not something that can be acquired. They help describe you, as well as influence your choices and actions. They help you understand why you're better at some things than others. These talents represent your innate power of potential.

But these *talents* can only become SWAGGER superpowers when you turn them into *strengths*.

Confused? You won't be for long. Stay with me, and I'll explain.

Strengths are created with practice over time. It is a collective process of using your *talents*, developing your *skills*, and building your base of *knowledge*.

These strengths are like recipes, only successful if you have all the right ingredients. First, you start with your talent—this is your main ingredient. Next, you add the ingredient of time, in the form of practice. Then, you need to practice and practice, using your talent in different contexts. Finally, you need to add the knowledge and specific skillsets that you have accumulated while you've practiced your talent.

To better understand the difference between *talents* and *strengths*, let's turn to the consulting firm, Gallup. Gallup are the prominent experts in strengths-based development and have been studying strengths in people across the globe for decades. Gallup defines *talent* as "a naturally recurring pattern of thought, feeling, or behavior that can be productively applied." Notice the focus on the words "naturally recurring," highlighting the fact that your talents are inherent and not something that can be learned. A *strength*, on the other hand, is defined as "the ability to consistently produce a positive outcome through near-perfect performance in a specific task."

To simplify it, just think of it like this: *talents* are a way of being, just part of who you are; *strengths* are what you develop over time by using and applying your talents to specific tasks.

Let me give you a couple of examples.

James is brilliant at putting himself in someone else's shoes, at sensing how other people feel—a talent that comes naturally to him and isn't something that he has to think about. James just happens to be a Cabin Service Director for British Airways and consistently provides his weary travelers with exactly what they need before they even ask for it. This ability is a strength that James has developed over time by applying his innate talent, developing his skills in service, and deepening his knowledge of the various needs that airline passengers might have.

Frida is exceptional at solving puzzles and seeing patterns that others don't even notice exist. This is a talent she possesses. Frida is also a travel agent, and seamlessly finds creative ways to provide her clients with cost-effective itineraries that have the fewest connections and maximize travel comfort. Frida manifested this strength by using her innate talent, developing her skills and network across the travel industry, and consistently increasing her knowledge of the latest programs and offers for each airline.

You can see how *talents*, combined with skills and knowledge, develop over time into *strengths*. And while all of the ingredients are required to create your strengths, it's your talent that is the most important. Why? Because your talents are innate and can't be learned. You can learn the latest programs for improving the fitness of your athletes. You can develop skills in reading offensive and defensive plays. But the ability to know how to get the best out of each one of your players is something that cannot be learned, and it's something that only exceptional team coaches inherently have.

The bottom line is this: you were born with innate potential—your greatest hits, your talents. These talents are unique to *you*. No one else has these exact talents. How do I know that? Research. Through research to develop the 34 talent themes as part of the CliftonStrengths® assessment, Gallup has proven that the chances of someone having the same top five talent themes as you are 1 in 277,000. The chances of someone having the exact top five talent themes in the same sequence as you are 1 in 33.4 million. These talents of yours are what you develop into your strengths and can ultimately become your exclusive and extraordinary SWAGGER superpowers.

When in Doubt

At this point, you might be thinking, "But I don't have any talents or strengths, and I certainly don't have any superpowers. What in the world is she going on about?"

Trust me, I understand completely. And as an example, I'll tell you that the character Harry Potter felt the same way. Check out this interaction below between Harry and the character of Moody, a "dark wizard catcher," from the book *Harry Potter and the Goblet of Fire* by J.K. Rowling:

"Play to your strengths," Moody said.

"I haven't got any," said Harry before he could stop himself.

"Excuse me," growled Moody, *"you've got strengths if I say you've got them. Think now. What are you best at?"*

I bring this up because Moody, here, is onto something. He asks Harry to think about what he is "best at." I am asking you to do the same thing. What are those tasks or activities that come easily to you, so much so that you can get lost in doing them and completely lose track of time? Those are clues to support the fact that you not only have talents, and subsequently strengths, but that you've also already been using them.

Actually, there are "five clues" identified by Gallup that exist to help you recognize when you're tapping into and using your talents and strengths, and these clues are listed below.

1. **Desire or Yearning**—activities that you are naturally drawn to
2. **Rapid Learning**—activities wherein you seem to pick things up quickly or remember extremely well
3. **Flow**—activities where you seem to already know the steps that need to be taken without being told what they are, where time

just slips away, and you don't even notice how long you've been working on or doing that activity

4. **Glimpses of Excellence**—activities where you've experienced moments of subconscious excellence, when you thought, "How did I do that?"

5. **Satisfaction**—activities that give you a sense of fulfillment, that fill you with energy so much that, when you finish, you think "Wow, when can I do that again?"

Let's see if I can use a few examples to bring these clues to life:

First, in regard to **Desire and Yearning**, we're usually drawn to things that we enjoy. We tend to enjoy tasks and activities that we're naturally good at doing. We're good at doing those activities because they enable us to utilize and tap into talents and strengths.

Let's take a look at Marc, who is a PhD candidate. Marc adores research, which is a good thing considering he's in the middle of completing his dissertation. He somehow can just pour into a topic and go hours upon hours sifting through endless information. Marc exhibits Input® and Context® as two of his top five dominant talent themes. Individuals with the Input® talent theme desire to know more. They love collecting and archiving all kinds of information. Individuals with the Context® talent theme enjoy thinking and learning about the past. They tend to create their understanding of the present by studying history. Doing research allows Marc to tap into both his Input® and Context® talent themes. This is why he loves it so much and has a constant desire and yearning for more.

What about incidences of **Rapid Learning**? A great example of this might be Alexa. Alexa is a leader and an exceptional problem solver. She is often referred to as a "fixer" for her ability to go into any existing project that is struggling and quickly figure out how to solve what is wrong. Alexa exhibits Restorative™ and Focus® in her top five dominant talent themes. Those who exhibit the Restorative™ talent theme are great at analyzing a situation, identifying potential shortcomings, and making necessary modifications. The Focus® talent theme also enables Alexa to remain realistic and practical, and to have the self-discipline to devote all her mental and physical energy to a particular job or assignment. These two talent themes together help Alexa get up to speed quickly on a problem, get a project back on track, and move everything in a positive direction. That's **Rapid Learning** at work.

Let's look at the next three together: **Flow**, **Glimpses of Excellence**, and **Satisfaction**. The example I always use here is actually a personal one, and I have to tell you that this isn't necessarily an activity that I love doing. However, it's a good illustration of these three clues in action. My husband and I have spent a lot of time renovating our house. He gains a lot of satisfaction from doing much of that work himself.

Specifically, when it comes to painting, he and I each have our specific roles. I tape it off, he does the bulk of the painting, and then I follow up with detailed touch-ups and fine tunings around areas like the crown molding, base, door frames, and windows. When it comes to **Flow**, I can spend literal hours on all of the most minute details, moving from one color to another to create clean lines, and even achieve perfection (or as close to it as I can get anyway). Before I know it, the whole day is gone and I'm still working. I even have moments when I touch up a spot and it comes out perfectly the first time around. "Wow," I say to myself, "how the heck did that happen?" This doesn't happen terribly often, mind you, but when it does, it's a demonstration of **Glimpses of Excellence**. Last, when I finally finish the long and arduous task of creating those clean, perfect lines, I feel a huge sense of **Satisfaction** at what I've accomplished.

Maximizer® and Achiever® are both in my top five talent themes. The Maximizer® talent theme keeps me focused on attaining perfection. Average and mediocre just won't do for me—they are not words that even exist in my vocabulary. The Achiever® talent theme, then, keeps me going on a particular thing until I finish it. It provides all the needed stamina to keep working until the task is completed. Now, I can't honestly say that I am looking forward to painting again any time soon, but this task does provide a strong example of some of my talents at work, as demonstrated by those three clues once again: **Flow, Glimpses of Excellence**, and **Satisfaction**.

So now it's your turn. Ask yourself what activities you can identify where any, several, or all of these clues might be present for you? What do you *desire* and *yearn* to do? When have you seen evidence of *learning rapidly*? What about the times when you have been in *flow*, seen *glimpses of excellence*, or achieved great *satisfaction*?

Give this all some careful thought and jot down a few ideas in a notebook . . .

And guess what? Believe it or not, you have just provided proof positive that you do indeed possess both talents and strengths, and that you've already been using them. Amazing, isn't it?

(Also, FYI, that comment about the notebook wasn't rhetorical. I would like you to actually capture the activities you identified. You'll need those responses later on for your practice.)

Getting to Know Your Talents

So now that you know you have talents (or your greatest hits), let's work on getting to know them a little better.

For this, we will once again turn to Gallup. So, as I briefly touched on above, through decades of research, they've been able to identify the talents most aligned with the potential for success and grouped them into 34 themes. This list of themes will enable you to further discover and explore your talents. As you read through them, you will find some that will more than likely resonate with you. But, for now, I'm going to ask you to be patient. I'll provide further guidance on how to uncover your *signature* talent themes a bit later. Consider this merely a preview of coming attractions.

Let's take a look:

ACHIEVER®	People exceptionally talented in the Achiever® theme work hard and possess a great deal of stamina. They take immense satisfaction in being busy and productive.
ACTIVATOR®	People exceptionally talented in the Activator® theme can make things happen by turning thoughts into action. They want to do things now, rather than simply talk about them.
ADAPTABILITY®	People exceptionally talented in the Adaptability® theme prefer to go with the flow. They tend to be "now" people who take things as they come and discover the future one day at a time.
ANALYTICAL®	People exceptionally talented in the Analytical® theme search for reasons and causes. They have the ability to think about all the factors that might affect a situation.
ARRANGER®	People exceptionally talented in the Arranger® theme can organize, but they also have a flexibility that complements this ability. They like to determine how all of the pieces and resources can be arranged for maximum productivity.
BELIEF®	People exceptionally talented in the Belief® theme have certain core values that are unchanging. Out of these values emerges a defined purpose for their lives.
COMMAND®	People exceptionally talented in the Command® theme have presence. They can take control of a situation and make decisions.
COMMUNICATION®	People exceptionally talented in the Communication® theme generally find it easy to put their thoughts into words. They are good conversationalists and presenters.
COMPETITION®	People exceptionally talented in the Competition® theme measure their progress against the performance of others. They strive to win first place and revel in contests.

CONNECTEDNESS®	People exceptionally talented in the Connectedness® theme have faith in the links among all things. They believe there are few coincidences and that almost every event has meaning.
CONSISTENCY®	People exceptionally talented in the Consistency® theme are keenly aware of the need to treat people the same. They try to treat everyone with equality by setting up clear rules and adhering to them.
CONTEXT®	People exceptionally talented in the Context® theme enjoy thinking about the past. They understand the present by researching its history.
DELIBERATIVE®	People exceptionally talented in the Deliberative® theme are best described by the serious care they take in making decisions or choices. They anticipate obstacles.
DEVELOPER®	People exceptionally talented in the Developer® theme recognize and cultivate the potential in others. They spot the signs of each small improvement and derive satisfaction from evidence of progress.
DISCIPLINE®	People exceptionally talented in the Discipline® theme enjoy routine and structure. Their world is best described by the order they create.
EMPATHY®	People exceptionally talented in the Empathy® theme can sense other people's feelings by imagining themselves in others' lives or situations.
FOCUS®	People exceptionally talented in the Focus® theme can take a direction, follow through, and make the corrections necessary to stay on track. They prioritize, then act.
FUTURISTIC®	People exceptionally talented in the Futuristic® theme are inspired by the future and what could be. They energize others with their visions of the future.

HARMONY®	People exceptionally talented in the Harmony® theme look for consensus. They don't enjoy conflict; rather, they seek areas of agreement.
IDEATION®	People exceptionally talented in the Ideation® theme are fascinated by ideas. They are able to find connections between seemingly disparate phenomena.
INCLUDER®	People exceptionally talented in the Includer® theme accept others. They show awareness of those who feel left out and make an effort to include them.
INDIVIDUALIZATION®	People exceptionally talented in the Individualization® theme are intrigued with the unique qualities of each person. They have a gift for figuring out how different people can work together productively.
INPUT®	People exceptionally talented in the Input® theme have a need to collect and archive. They may accumulate information, ideas, artifacts, or even relationships.
INTELLECTION®	People exceptionally talented in the Intellection® theme are characterized by their intellectual activity. They are introspective and appreciate intellectual discussions.
LEARNER®	People exceptionally talented in the Learner® theme have a great desire to learn and want to continuously improve. The process of learning, rather than the outcome, excites them.
MAXIMIZER®	People exceptionally talented in the Maximizer® theme focus on strengths as a way to stimulate personal and group excellence. They seek to transform something strong into something superb.
POSITIVITY®	People especially talented in the Positivity® theme have contagious enthusiasm. They are upbeat and can get others excited about what they are going to do.

RELATOR®	People exceptionally talented in the Relator® theme enjoy close relationships with others. They find deep satisfaction in working hard with friends to achieve a goal.
RESPONSIBILITY®	People exceptionally talented in the Responsibility® theme take psychological ownership of what they say they will do. They are committed to stable values such as honesty and loyalty.
RESTORATIVE™	People exceptionally talented in the Restorative® theme are adept at dealing with problems. They are good at figuring out what is wrong and resolving it.
SELF–ASSURANCE®	People exceptionally talented in the Self–Assurance® theme feel confident in their ability to manage their own lives. They have an inner compass that gives them certainty in their decisions.
SIGNIFICANCE®	People exceptionally talented in the Significance® theme want to make a big impact. They are independent and prioritize projects based on how much influence they will have on their organization or people around them.
STRATEGIC®	People exceptionally talented in the Strategic® theme create alternative ways to proceed. Faced with any given scenario, they can quickly spot the relevant patterns and issues.
WOO®	People exceptionally talented in the Woo® theme love the challenge of meeting new people and winning them over. They derive satisfaction from breaking the ice and making a connection with someone.

A couple of things to remember when looking at these talent themes:

First, they are neutral, impartial, and unbiased. They are what they are. Themes aren't meant to be used as labels. You are not *an* Achiever®, but you might *have* Achiever® as one of your dominant talent themes. Does that make sense?

Second, keep your focus on the positive, and look for what's great about possessing whatever talent theme you've identified. In this chapter, we will explore how talent themes can have a downside, but that'll come a bit later.

Last, keep in mind that your talent themes help describe what makes you special, what makes you different from others, and how those differences can be to your distinct advantage.

Gallup has further categorized the 34 talent themes by grouping them into "domains." This can further help you understand your own personal talent themes by enabling you to think about how your talents can help you get things done, influence others, build relationships, and how you process information.

Take a look at how the 34 themes are arranged within the four domains. Again, they are only meant to further support you in identifying how your themes show up in everyday activities.

EXECUTING	INFLUENCING	RELATIONSHIP BUILDING	STRATEGIC THINKING
People with dominant Executing themes know how to make things happen.	People with dominant Influencing themes take charge, speak up, and make sure others are heard.	People with dominant Relationship Building themes build strong relationships that can hold a team together and make it greater than the sum of its parts.	People with dominant Strategic Thinking themes absorb and analyze information that informs better decisions.
Achiever® Arranger® Belief® Consistency® Deliberative® Discipline® Focus® Responsibility® Restorative™	Activator® Command® Communication® Competition® Maximizer® Self-Assurance® Significance® Woo®	Adaptability® Connectedness® Developer® Empathy® Harmony® Includer® Individualization® Positivity® Relator®	Analytical® Context® Futuristic® Ideation® Input® Intellection® Learner® Strategic®

To reiterate, these talent theme domains are meant to help you better understand your specific talent themes—*period*. They aren't meant to seem limiting, disheartening, or in any way suggest that you're unable to perform any types of activities that do or don't exist within particular domains.

For example, if your dominant talent themes fall under "Relationship Building" and "Influencing" domains, it doesn't mean that you're incapable of strategic thinking or getting things done. Don't worry! You can, of course, successfully perform your role as the Head of Strategy for your organization even if your dominant talent themes don't fall within the "Strategic Thinking" domain.

Likewise, if you have dominant themes in "Executing" and "Strategic Thinking" domains, you can still be exceptionally good at building relationships and influencing people. You can be the best Head of HR your company has ever seen, even if your dominant themes don't sit under the

"Relationship Building" domain. This is all simply information, and I want to encourage you to use it as such.

Let's explore this concept further.

Making the Most of What You Have

Your talents don't work singularly in isolation, but rather they work in combination with one another.

Let me give you an example. Most people who meet me don't believe that I'm actually an introvert, which, unfortunately, has everything to do with how that word is defined. I define an individual as "introvert" when they get their energy from within, or from solitude, not from being around other people.

Of course, now you might be wondering how an introvert becomes a global leadership consultant who has to meet with new clients and deliver workshops to large groups of leaders all over the world all year long. How can I, as an introvert, be effective in such a role? You are probably thinking that an individual who would excel as a global leadership consultant would actually benefit greatly if they exhibited Woo® or Communication® themes as part of their dominant talents.

By Gallup's definition, Woo® is actually an acronym that stands for "**w**inning **o**thers **o**ver." People who possess the Woo® talent theme thrive on the challenge of meeting new people and get satisfaction from making new connections. Subsequently, people with the Communication® talent theme find it easy to put their thoughts into words and are skillful conversationalists or presenters.

So, if you look at *my* dominant talent themes, Woo® and Communication® are nowhere near my top five, and, in fact, are not even in my top ten. Woo® sits at an astounding number 32 out of 34, and Communication® is at 22 out of 34 in my overall talent themes report. However, I still manage to perform well in a role that requires engaging with new people and exceptional communication skills.

How?

Well, the answer lies within my specific talents and how I use them. See, my top five talent themes are Maximizer®, Relator®, Strategic®, Individualization®, and Achiever®. The Relator® talent helps me use my inherent authenticity to build close connections with others to foster trust and confidence. Then, the Strategic® talent enables me to read a room and quickly determine what each individual in said room might need from me to build a connection. Finally, Individualization® helps me see the uniqueness of each new person and identify what I can do to bring out their best. These three talents *in combination with one another* are the special sauce that helps me succeed in this role. They support me whether I am meeting new clients for the first time or delivering a workshop to a room full of leaders.

Pretty interesting, right? In the end, am I able to communicate well without possessing Communication® as one of my dominant talent themes? Let's look again at the Strategic® and Individualization® talents. Together, these talents enable me to adjust key messages in different ways to meet new people where they are. I'm able to make complex ideas seem simple and bring theory into reality. Granted, it's not a one-size-fits-all approach, but my talents ensure that each person receives the information in a way that speaks to them. Additionally, Responsibility®, Self-Assurance®, and Belief® are all in my top 10 talent themes. With the Responsibility® talent, I have a deep sense of dedication and ownership for what I do. Self-Assurance® gives me the ability to lead with certainty, even in high-risk situations. With the Belief® talent, I provide clarity, conviction, and stability by believing in what I do and living my values. These three talents, also working in combination with one another, create an environment where people trust me, have confidence in what I say, and are willing to let me lead them on a developmental journey. So, even though I don't possess two key talents that you might think are necessary for success in a role like global leadership consultant, this shows you that it's not about what I *don't have* at all. Instead, it's about making the most of what I do have.

Now, let's assess what this means for you. The same holds true: by focusing on what you're naturally good at, you can develop your talents into strengths and use your SWAGGER superpowers to create success in any of your roles in life.

Too Much of a Good Thing

Remember when I said that we'd take a look at how your talent themes can have a downside?

Well, here we go.

Just as in life, too much of a good thing is simply just that—too much. How does that relate to your talents, strengths, and SWAGGER superpowers? Let's take a look at the visual example below, featuring two "professors"—Rose and Blue—and how others might perceive them.

Professor Rose	Professor Blue
Is known for being upbeat, having contagious enthusiasm, and getting others excited about what they're doing	Can be seen as being naïve, unrealistic, and not grounded in reality
Is recognized for cultivating the potential in others, and loves seeing progress no matter how small	Is perceived by some as being too soft, wasting time with low performers
Is great at organizing and seeing how all the resources can work together for the best productivity	Is constantly making rearrangements to the team, and seems to get bored easily
Focuses on ensuring that no one is left out	Lacks a high-performance mindset, can be indiscriminate
Craves information, always seems to want to know more	Takes too long to make decisions, can overload others with too much information

So, now, having gone over that, what do you notice? What strikes you about Professor Rose and Professor Blue?

If you haven't guessed, they're the same person. What you see listed under "Professor Rose" are what would be considered "positive attributes," or the upsides of a top five dominant talent themes featuring Positivity®, Developer®, Arranger®, Includer®, and Input®. What's listed under "Professor Blue," then, is how these talents, when overused, can become barriers.

Even though any of these talents are always part of our greatest hits, and are what help create SWAGGER superpowers, when they're overused, they can be perceived by others as negative, not positive.

You might say that our SWAGGER superpowers should come with a warning label:

Warning!
Use with focus and intentionality.
May cause damage if misused or overused.

Your talents—and, by virtue, your SWAGGER superpowers—when overused, or simply misused, can undermine your ability to succeed. They can even become what could be called a *weakness*. Gallup defines weakness as "something that gets in the way of success." In their strengths-based approach, weakness is defined as "a shortage or misapplication of talent, skill, or knowledge that causes problems for you or others."

The thing is every upside has a downside. Once identified and honed, your SWAGGER superpowers can't be used haphazardly. You must take the time to develop these superpowers and learn to use them effectively. More than that, you also have to recognize the warning signs and triggers that alert you to when you're overusing or misusing your superpowers and they begin to get in the way of your success.

Now I know what you're going to ask.

"Jennifer, how do I know when my SWAGGER superpowers are getting in my way or being overused?"

Well, see, that's the hardest part—often you don't. I mean you probably don't wake up in the morning thinking you're going to overuse your strengths, or that you're going to intentionally frustrate or upset those you lead, like coworkers, family, or friends. Sadly, even with the best intentions, this can happen more than you think.

For instance, perhaps Strategic® is one of your top five talent themes. Over time, you harness this talent into a superpower. You're quick to see patterns, how all the pieces fit together, and can lay out a clear path forward far faster than anyone else around you. You see this talent as a positive, as a superpower—the ability to chart the course ahead. But instead of creating a positive outcome as expected, this superpower generates a drop in engagement and productivity. Why? Well, because those working around you feel like you've left them behind. They feel like they can't keep up with you. They often don't even understand where you want them to go, or how they're going to get there.

Perhaps you have Analytical® in your top five talent themes. You pride yourself on making sure that you have all of the information before making decisions. In your mind, this ensures that you're making the best choices possible, minimizing errors and mistakes in the process. The impact of this on those around you actually manifests as frustration and lack of confidence. They feel like it takes forever to get decisions made. They see you as being indecisive, which creates a lack of confidence in the ultimate decision made and the ability to execute on it.

Maybe it's Developer® that's in your top five. You have honed this talent to a superpower to become a *super*-developer of others. You love helping people grow, progress, and improve. You naturally zero in on individuals who need and could benefit from your help the most, because this is where you feel you can make the greatest difference. However, this superpower produces the unintended impact of a decrease in engagement, performance quality, and productivity. The people around you feel like you spend too much time focused on low performers, and, as such, that your performance expectations are too low. Why should they bother to do high-quality work when your focus is always on helping those who need to improve?

Each of the three above examples highlight an unintentional overuse or misuse of a SWAGGER superpower, and you're probably thinking, "Great, here you tell me I have SWAGGER superpowers, but now you say that even when I have the best intentions, I can still make a mess of things when I use them. What exactly am I supposed to do?"

I get it. But hang on.

First, don't panic. Just like in many aspects of life, the development of SWAGGER superpowers is all about balance. The challenge here is that you might not often recognize when you're misusing these superpowers. But there's a simple remedy to this, by asking the right questions and utilizing the help of those around you. Let those you work with and those who know you best become your mirror. Take inventory from them, by asking "What should I do more of? What should I do less of? What should I keep doing?"

Second, be open to *receiving* information. Remember that, if you've asked those around you for their help, they aren't criticizing you when they respond, they're helping you see what you maybe have not been able to. If what you hear from them doesn't make sense to you in the moment, then ask for more information. Ask for examples to help illustrate what they mean. The more clarity you can glean about what they've said, the greater the chances are that you can alter your behavior and more effectively use your SWAGGER superpowers going forward.

Third, when the information is processed, be willing to work on taking action to adjust your behavior. Just because you have all the best intentions doesn't always mean you'll get it right every time. Intentions alone don't equate to effective execution. Really, it's about fine-tuning, and trial and error.

It's also about agility. You might need to use your SWAGGER superpowers in one way based on that particular setting and environment, but another situation might require a different approach. Additionally, you can't forget about all your other SWAGGER superpowers. Are you able to lean in to one of your other superpowers to help you fine-tune one you're currently using, overusing, or misusing? Taking the time to hone all of these superpowers means developing the ability to adapt and adjust to your situations and surroundings.

Let's look at our three examples again.

If Strategic® is one of your top talent themes and you tend to move too quickly, potentially leaving people behind, it might be as easy as asking more questions. By asking more questions, you can ensure that people are tracking along with you, that they know where they're going, and that they understand the part they play.

If Analytical® is in your top five and you tend to take too long to make decisions, you might consider creating specific deadlines for each decision. That way, everyone knows exactly when the decision will be made. You might also need to encourage yourself to get better at doing the best you can with limited information. This can be challenging and will take time to become more comfortable with, because even though we live in a world where information is at our fingertips, it's difficult to feel like you have all of the information you need. Sometimes you just need to take a deep breath and do the best you can with what you have to work with.

If Developer® is one of your top themes and people feel like you spend too much time with low performers, perhaps it's as simple as setting up regular one-on-one meetings with each person you're working with. Setting aside this time with each individual and asking questions to uncover what they need from you helps people feel like they matter and that you're there to support everyone, not just the people you think need your help the most.

Once you know more about what it looks like when you overuse or misuse your SWAGGER superpowers, you will be able to encourage those around you to help keep you on track. For instance, I know that I get super picky and overly focused on perfection when I am under tight deadlines or time constraints or working on a high-profile project. "Can't you see that those images are not lined up on the page?" I might say to people working with me. "Can't you see that the font is different in those two paragraphs? Can't you see the misspelled words?" I could go on and on, and I recognize that the environment can get really intense and others feel like I'm attacking their work. But it isn't attacking people or their work, truly. It's my Maximizer® superpower in overdrive. And this is something I know about myself, so I let people on my project teams know that this is something that will likely happen. I ask that they please alert me when it does happen, so I can adjust. They'll say, "Hey, Jennifer, you're doing that [Maximizer® *thing*] again." Not only does it allow me the opportunity to stop and reframe and reapproach, but also, this way there is open communication through the project life cycle, and we can all work together to minimize frustration on the team and keep things moving forward in a positive direction.

Last, whatever happens, I implore you not to abandon the use of your SWAGGER superpowers based on the fear that you might overuse or misuse them. You aren't going to stop driving a car just because you might get into an accident. Chefs aren't going to stop using kitchen knives because they might accidentally cut themselves. Firefighters won't stop themselves from rushing into a flaming inferno because they might get burned. You, and those in the instances above, all have a healthy respect for the danger that's involved in doing what needs to be done. You can still drive your car and uncover new adventures, chefs can still work to create culinary masterpieces, and firefighters can keep tapping into their courage to help save lives.

The same holds true for your SWAGGER superpowers. Don't stop using them just because there could be mistakes made along the way. In this case, you are the adventure waiting to be uncovered, the culinary masterpiece waiting to be created, the victim in the inferno waiting to be saved. Writer, poet, and philosopher, Gugu Mona, said it best: "Remember that a rose does not hide its beauty due to the prickles around it. So, never allow weaknesses to stop you from embracing your strengths."

It's important to remember that you're a work in progress. Life is all about progress, not perfection. So let's dive into the innate potential you were born with, harness your talents, develop them into strengths, and ultimately into extraordinary SWAGGER superpowers. Don't be afraid to use what is uniquely yours. Embrace and celebrate your SWAGGER superpowers. Use them to help claim your SWAGGER and become who you were born to be.

Time to Start Doing

This chapter has been all about gaining appreciation for your strengths and limitations, but to do that, it means you have to discover your talents, gain awareness of how and where they show up, learn to develop them into strengths and, ultimately, SWAGGER superpowers.

Well, now it's time to stop talking, or in this case, stop reading, and start doing. The following activities will provide a guide to help you get started.

Developing your SWAGGER superpowers is not one-and-done, not simply some task you check off your list. Developing, and then mastering, your SWAGGER superpowers takes **P to the Power of 3 – Patience – Practice – Perseverance**. So, first things first, you will have to be patient with yourself. Mistakes will happen, and this will take time. Be willing to keep practicing. The more you practice effectively using your SWAGGER superpowers, the better you'll be at wielding them. Don't give up. Just keep at it, and you'll see how your perseverance pays off in the long run.

As you start to uncover your talents, I encourage you to reread certain parts of this chapter. Once you have a better understanding of those greatest hits—those talents, strengths, and superpowers—the concepts discussed here will take on even more meaning. Revisit this chapter as often as you like.

Finally, don't forget to have fun along the way. Enjoy this journey of self-discovery.

Well? Are you ready? Okay, then, let's get to it.

Activity: Discovering Your Greatest Hits
Time: 30 minutes

It's time to discover the potential you were born with, your greatest hits, your unique talents. Are you excited? You should be. This information will unlock a whole new world for you, a whole new understanding of who you are and how you show up.

Step 1

Go to swaggeru.com/my_swagger and access the link to purchase the CliftonStrengths® online talent assessment. You have two options. Option one: to uncover your top 5 talents. Option Two: discover your complete list of 34 talents. The choice is yours. Review the options and benefits of the two reports and determine what suits you best. Both assessments will provide insight into what makes you unique, and how to start using your talents to build strengths and your SWAGGER superpowers.

Step 2

Make sure to set aside about thirty minutes to an hour of uninterrupted time to complete the assessment. Yes, I mean uninterrupted time. The assessment is the same regardless of what reporting option you choose. You'll be responding to 177 paired statements and determining which ones fit you best. The assessment is timed, and you can't go back to revisit a previous answer. Go with your first instincts. Don't second guess yourself. This is about you and what makes you unique. There are no wrong answers, just your answers. When you're ready with your uninterrupted time and in a quiet place where you can think, take the assessment.

Step 3

Review your results. Read through your customized reports and be prepared to be amazed. If you are like any of the people I've worked with, you'll be asking: "How did they do that? How do they know me so well?" To answer your questions, it's because Gallup has assessed over 25 million people, so they have this down to a science, literally. Additionally, you were the one who responded to the statements. So it's you that knows you so well. Gallup has simply compiled your responses into a narrative that helps you make sense of your unique talents.

Activity: Connecting with Your Greatest Hits
Time: 20–30 minutes

Now that you've taken the assessment and read through your reports, it's time to home in on the words and phrases that resonate most with you. Before you can develop your greatest hits into strengths, you must first be able to identify with them, to see yourself in the talents you were born with. Sometimes this is easy, and other times it takes a bit more effort and the help of those who know you best.

Step 1
Reread your customized reports. This time highlight or record the words and phrases that resonate most with you for each talent theme.
Example taken from my CliftonStrengths® 34 Results report:

Maximizer®
Driven by your talents, you are aware of what you do naturally and well. You prefer to leverage your talents rather than spend time trying to overcome your shortcomings.
You expect excellence from yourself and others. Being average at best and mediocre at worst is unacceptable to you.
You focus on quality, and you prefer working with and for the best. By seeing what each person naturally does best and empowering them to do it, you make individuals, teams, and groups better.

Note: as you reread your reports, you might find a section or one of your talent themes that doesn't feel like you. That's OK. Share the report with a person who knows you exceptionally well, a partner, spouse, brother, sister, coworker, etc. Chances are that person will read the report and say, "That's totally you." What this illustrates is a talent that you demonstrate often to others, but you might be unaware of. Ask this person to share some examples of where they've seen this talent theme in you. Take notes on what they say. This will help you create greater awareness of this talent that might sit in your blind spot.

Step 2

Find the list of activities I asked you to jot down where you observed the five clues to tapping into your strengths: Desire, Rapid Learning, Flow, Glimpses of Excellence, and Satisfaction. Complete the following for each activity you listed.

- Which of the five clues were present in that activity?
- Identify your top talent themes that showed up in that activity.
- Describe how each of your top talent themes supported you in that activity.

Step 3

Identify a specific challenge you're facing, or a goal you're working toward. How can you tap into your top talents to support you with that challenge or goal? How are you currently using your talents, and what can you do to use them more effectively?

Daily Reinforcement: Shining a Light
Time: 5–10 minutes

This daily reinforcement is about raising your awareness of how your SWAGGER superpowers support you in your daily life. The more you realize *how* your SWAGGER superpowers support you, the more effective you'll become at employing them.

Step 1

Find a quiet place to sit down. Close your eyes and listen to your breath. On the inhale, say quietly to yourself, "Inhale." On the exhale, say quietly to yourself, "Exhale." Do this for one minute to clear and calm your mind.

Step 2

Think of a task, project, or situation you were faced with today. Perhaps you led a meeting or a call, had a conversation with one of your kids, helped a friend in need, or made a difficult decision.

Step 3

Capture the SWAGGER superpowers you used in this task, project, or situation. Next to each SWAGGER superpower, record how it supported or helped you.

Example: "Making a difficult decision"

Superpower	How
Strategic®	Helped me explore multiple options to come up with the best path forward.
Futuristic®	Helped me envision the impact of the decision.

Daily Reinforcement: Affirming Questions
Time: 3–5 minutes

Let's build on the idea of affirmations that we used in the previous chapter. Instead of just creating statements, you're going to craft constructive and empowering questions designed to help reprogram your beliefs, challenge negativity, and solidify mindset shifts. Best-selling author, speaker, and peak performance coach Noah St. John calls these Afformations®. His Afformations® Method is centered around the idea that your subconscious responds better to questions than it does to statements that you might not yet believe. There are three keys to creating success with affirming questions.

1. Write questions that align with what you desire to achieve or accomplish. These questions need to be meaningful for you. You won't have success with questions that mean something to someone else.
2. Set them in the present. Your questions need to include "why is it" not "how great would it be."
3. Say them with conviction. You have to ask these questions with belief. Your mind will respond better to a question asked with confidence, as if you already know the answer.

Step 1

Craft a list of affirming questions related to your SWAGGER superpowers. Below is a list to get you started.

- Why is it so easy for me to be exceptionally good at many things?
- How great is it that I have superpowers that are unique to me?
- Why is it so effortless for me to tap into and use what I'm good at daily?
- How fantastic is it that I was born with these amazing superpowers?
- How comforting is it to know that no one can take these superpowers away?

Step 2

Print out your list of affirming questions and place them by your bed. Ask your questions first thing in the morning when you wake up and right before you go to sleep at night. It might also be helpful to say your affirming questions anytime you find yourself in a challenging situation.

SWAGGER Insight

- You have SWAGGER superpowers that develop from your strengths.
- Strengths-based development suggests that peak productivity can be gained simply by focusing on and developing your strengths while being aware of and managing your weaknesses.
- You were born with talents, which are the way you inherently think, feel, and behave.
- Talents are things that come naturally to you and are not something that can be acquired.
- Your *talents* can only become your SWAGGER superpowers when you develop them into *strengths*.
- *Strengths* are created with practice over time. It is a collective process of using your *talents*, developing your *skills*, and building your base of *knowledge*.
- Gallup defines *talent* as a naturally recurring pattern of thoughts, feeling, or behavior that can be productively applied.
- Gallup defines a *strength* as the ability to consistently produce a positive outcome through near-perfect performance in a specific task.
- *Talents* are a way of being, just part of who you are; *strengths* are what you develop over time by using and applying your talents to specific tasks.
- The bottom line is this: you were born with innate potential—your greatest hits, your talents. These talents are unique to *you*. No one else has these exact talents.
- These talents of yours are what you develop into your strengths and can ultimately become your exclusive and extraordinary SWAGGER superpowers.
- The activities that come easily to you and that you can get lost in are clues to your talents and strengths.
- Gallup identified "five clues" that help you recognize when you're

tapping into and using your talents and strengths:
- o Desire or Yearning
- o Rapid Learning
- o Flow
- o Glimpses of Excellence
- o Satisfaction

- Through decades of research, Gallup identified 34 talent themes most aligned with the potential for success.
- Talent themes are neutral, impartial, and unbiased.
- Talent themes are not labels.
- Your talent themes help describe what makes you special, what makes you different from others, and how those differences can be to your distinct advantage.
- Gallup further categorized the 34 talent themes into four domains—Executing, Influencing, Relationship Building, and Strategic Thinking.
- These domains enable you to think about how your talents can help you get things done, influence others, build relationships, and how you process information.
- Talent theme domains don't dictate your ability to perform any type of activity that does or doesn't exist within particular domains.
- Your talents don't work singularly in isolation, but rather they work in combination with one another.
- It's not about focusing on what talents you don't have. Instead, it's about making the most of the talents you do have.
- By focusing on what you're naturally good at, you can develop your talents into strengths and use your SWAGGER superpowers to create success in any of your roles in life.
- When your talents are overused, they can be perceived by others as negative, not positive.
- Your SWAGGER superpowers should be used with focus and intentionality. They may cause damage if misused or overused.
- Your SWAGGER superpowers, when overused, can become a

weakness, which Gallup defines as something that gets in the way of success.

- Sometimes it's difficult to recognize when your SWAGGER superpowers are being overused or misused.

- To help minimize the impact of overusing or misusing your SWAGGER superpowers, you can enlist the help of others, ask questions, be open to receiving the requested information, and possess a willingness to adjust your behavior.

- Using your SWAGGER superpowers requires agility and the ability to adapt your approach based on the particular setting and environment.

- Don't stop using your SWAGGER superpowers just because there could be mistakes made along the way.

- Remember that you're a work in progress.

- Life is all about progress, not perfection.

- Developing your SWAGGER superpowers takes **P to the Power of 3 – Patience – Practice – Perseverance**.

- Be patient with yourself, mistakes will happen, and this will take time.

- Don't give up—your perseverance will pay off in the long run.

CHAPTER 5

Finding Gratitude for Your Life Experiences

f you had a chance to go back and change anything in your life, what would it be? You know, like in those movies where a lead character gets to go back in time and relive a moment, but does it differently that time around?

What moment in your own life would you choose? Why?

In the movies, it's always interesting because when the main character does go back, things don't always turn out as they thought they would. In fact, the experiences they have going back in time often help them generate a sense of appreciation for the life they *were* leading already, instead of the one they thought that they wanted.

The lesson here is one of gratitude.

But what if I told you that finding gratitude for the life you have doesn't require going back in time to figure out? What if you could simply revisit your life experiences, not to relive them or change them, but to learn from them? Well, you can, and that's exactly what this chapter will help you do.

Feeling excited right now? Scared? Don't fret. I've seen firsthand the transformative power this work generates. Let's see if we can reduce some of that fear by increasing your level of understanding. Before we dig into how to go about doing this, let's first focus on why this is a crucial aspect to claiming your SWAGGER.

You're a Product of Your Past

Recently my dad asked me if there was anything I would change about my past. What he was really asking, though, was if there was anything that he and my mother, as my parents, could've done differently.

I gave this some careful thought and replied, "Honestly, no. I don't think you could've or should've done anything differently. Our past helps shape who we are today, and each experience has a place and lesson for us on our journey. If I'd skipped any of those, I wouldn't be the person I am today."

Now, by saying that, it certainly doesn't mean that I'd want to go back and *repeat* some of those experiences, mind you. It just means I'm grateful for what I've learned and how I've grown as a result of those experiences. I know that all the things I've experienced in my past have made me who I am today.

When my husband and I first started dating, he would ask me questions about my past—as you do when you're trying to learn about someone. I remember asking him in return, "Do you love me?" When he replied, "Yes," I said, "Then you love my past as well because my past helped make me who I am. And sometimes the past needs to be left in the past."

While there are times to reflect on, learn from, and perhaps even share your past, there are also other times where you just have to let the past go.

Now let's look at this through a different lens.

Ever watched a movie or TV show and developed an extreme dislike for one of the characters? But as you continue to watch, and more infor-mation is revealed about that character and their past, you suddenly have a deeper understanding of why they behave the way they do. It's the realization that the character has been shaped by their experiences, and how they *are behaving* is informed by what happened to them in the past.

Walt Disney Pictures provided two great opportunities to look into the history of popular characters we thought we knew. Maleficent was the evil and powerful sorceress that placed a curse on Princess Aurora in 1959's *Sleeping Beauty*. But the recent hit movie *Maleficent*, we're given new information. We learn that Maleficent wasn't born evil. She had idyllic beginnings as a beautiful, pure-hearted fairy who was the protector of others. It was the ruthless betrayal by someone she loved that turned her heart to stone and shaped her behavior going forward. Similarly, we were also shown that Cruella de Vil, the villain from *101 Dalmatians*, wasn't born wicked and vicious after all. In the 2021 film *Cruella*, we learn that she wasn't actually born "Cruella" at all. Her name was Estella, a child constantly teased for her black and white hair and orphaned at the age of 12. The events and revelations she experienced in her quest to become a fashionista caused Estella to embrace her wickedness and unleash "Cruella."

Both of these examples highlight the enormous impact life experiences have on shaping how you show up in your life today, and who you choose to be.

So how does this happen? How do your past experiences shape who you are, exactly? The best way to understand this is to focus on how the brain works—don't worry, you won't need a neuroscience degree to comprehend it.

Think of your brain as a vast filing system. Every experience you have from the time you're born is a piece of information that your brain files away. Your brain works to categorize these experiences. As something new is experienced, the brain analyzes it, assessing whether it can be filed into a pre-existing category, or if a new category altogether needs to be created.

For example, your early experiences with parents or caregivers might be filed into a "relationship" category. Over time, then, your brain might add subcategories like "family," "friendships," and "romance." You might have numerous other categories for "food," or "sports," or "skills," or "travel.". Your brain is constantly categorizing your experiences every day, so you can imagine the infinite number of categories that exist inside. Then, for every experience categorized, your brain will also log information about the situation, who or what was involved, how you felt, the emotions it elicited, and the meaning you assigned to it.

Let's look at two examples to help illustrate this concept.

In the first, a baby smiles at an adult caregiver. The baby then receives a smile in return, along with additional nurturing and comforting affection. Chemicals released in the brain cause the baby to feel happy, safe, and loved. The brain categorizes the positive emotion associated with this experience, increasing the likelihood of the baby repeating that action of smiling in the future.

In the second situation, a baby smiles at an adult caregiver and they receive nothing in response. No smile and no additional affection in return. The adult caregiver simply walks away, leaving the baby uncertain and alone. The baby feels a sense of anxiety and stress instead of happiness, safety, and love. The brain categorizes that negative emotion associated with the experience, which then decreases the likelihood that the baby will repeat that behavior going forward.

See how our past experiences can impact our future behavior?

Now, of course these are rudimentary examples used to illustrate a concept, however, there are countless studies that demonstrate the direct connection between how the brain records and categorizes experience and the subsequent elicited behavior.

So why does the brain do this?

Your brain works this way to help you make sense of and figure out how to engage with the world around you. Your brain's vast catalog of past experiences holds the keys to why you behave the way you do *today*. If, for example, you were raised in an environment of hunger and scarcity, you might find yourself always compelled to "stock up," intensely focused on never running out of anything. If you experienced a burglary when you were younger, you might nowadays find yourself hypervigilant about securing your home and loved ones. Or if you grew up in a household where someone you trusted violated that trust, you might find it difficult, if not impossible, to trust other people in your life.

The important thing here is to recognize that you are a product of your past, and that these past experiences form the framework for who you are and who you will become. To truly claim your SWAGGER, you must take the time to explore and examine how these events in your life have helped shape who you are and, ultimately, how you show up.

Most importantly, I'm sure you're asking, "But, Jennifer, what can I *learn* from these experiences?"

What experiences from your past do you need to learn from? What do you need to let go of? Will you choose to discover gratitude for how those many experiences have helped you grow and develop, or will you continue to let yourself be defined by them?

There are so many questions to answer, I understand. But not just yet. First, let's peel back a few more layers and take a closer look at your brain.

The Path of Least Resistance

Without consciously realizing it, your brain is automatically categorizing every situation you encounter based on your previous experiences.

Let me say that again: your brain automatically categorizes new information based on your previous experiences.

Now, let's reflect on that for a brief moment.

As your brain collects and categorizes this information, it creates the foundation for your patterns of behavior. It does this by using neural pathways to communicate information and create behavioral responses. Over time, your brain strengthens and works to optimize the most commonly used neural pathways. The stronger, and more worn, a pathway becomes, the more ingrained the resulting pattern of behavior is. Does that make sense?

Great, then, would you like the good news or bad news first?

Alright, here's the good news. This process enables you to create deep subject-matter expertise and supports your self-preservation and survival in this crazy world.

For example, if you're hiking in the woods and you come across bear tracks going in the same direction you are, what are you going to do? That's right. The experience information collected in your brain would tell you to not walk, but run in the opposite direction. Better that than ending up at lunch with a bear—or being lunch for that matter!

Okay, if you've got a handle on that, now the bad news.

Well, wait, instead of "bad" news, let's call it "challenging news." The *challenging* news is, as your brain matures, its heavily used neural pathways become more and more entrenched, which makes the corresponding patterns of behavior to those pathways become that much more defined, and therefore, harder to break free from and change.

But notice that I said "harder," not "impossible."

See, your brain likes to take the worn and familiar path. In essence, your brain follows "the path of least resistance." It's why the saying "you can't teach an old dog new tricks" exists. The reality is, you can learn and create new behaviors at any age. However, it gets much more difficult to do that as you mature, after your neural pathways begin to solidify, which is around the age of 25.

Not only do neural pathways solidify, but your brain actually loses flexibility and plasticity as you age. It's why you become, what some would call, "set in your ways." Neuroscientists, however, would say that you have "low neuroplasticity." Although it's disappointing, when you think about it, why would your brain build a whole brand-new highway when there's a perfectly good one already in use? It'd be like trying to build a new freeway in Los Angeles during rush hour instead of just taking the express lane, which is wide open, and traffic is flowing freely.

Which would you choose? Exactly.

So right now, you're probably wondering, "What does any of this have to do with my life experiences?"

Stick with me here.

When you have a better understanding of how your brain works, and how it categorizes your new experiences and forms your new patterns of behavior as a result of those experiences, you begin to realize how important your past life experiences actually are—and not just the experiences themselves, but the *meaning* you assign to them.

The pathways that begin to form in your brain in your youth tend to stay with you and shape your behavior for a long time. That means that how you view those previous life experiences, and the stories you tell yourself about them, becomes increasingly significant to who you are now.

Are things starting to become clear?

The Stories You Tell

What do I mean when I say, "the stories you tell yourself"? Sounds a bit strange, doesn't it?

Think of it like this: you are the screenwriter for the movie of your life. As the screenwriter, you describe the emotions associated with all of the experiences that take place in that movie. The meaning you assign to those experiences determines how the memories based on those experiences are stored and the impact they ultimately have on you, the main character, going forward.

These stories that you tell yourself will directly impact your current mindset, confidence, and self-worth. They create a lens through which you view and interact with the world around you. They are what helps shape your behaviors, choices, and actions.

But instead of me trying to describe this concept further, I think it's best to explore it through a few examples.

Sandra is a young married woman with one child who's highly focused on her career. Her parents divorced when she was a teenager, and it was a difficult time for her. The story she told herself about that divorce went like this: "You can't trust your partner. Marriage is not necessarily forever. Things can happen, and you might find yourself having to figure it out alone. You should always be prepared to take care of yourself. You can't rely on anyone else."

This story that Sandra told herself continues to guide her to this day. She's fiercely independent. She kept her maiden name, "just in case," as she says, and she's an extreme DIY-er, attempting to fix everything herself, without anyone's help. Now, this is not to say that she doesn't value her marriage or want it to succeed. But when she's faced with decisions, Sandra defaults to what will best support her career and her ability to take care of herself and her child.

Jack served in the United States Army for many years, much of that time spent in the Special Forces. He was injured in Afghanistan and had his left leg amputated as a result. The story Jack told himself about this injury was this: "I owe it to those who've fallen to live life to the fullest. I survived. I must make the most of this gift when it's been denied to so many others."

The story Jack began telling himself carries enormous weight and power. He didn't dwell on what happened to him. The meaning he assigned to that experience propelled him forward and continues to drive him today. As a speaker, he shares his message of overcoming adversity. He's the founder of multiple companies that donate portions of their prof-its to charities that support military members, veterans, first responders, and their families.

So in both of these examples, the story each person told themselves about a specific experience in their life stayed the same. Good or bad, the meaning they assigned to these experiences continues to guide them in their lives today. Sometimes, though, the story you tell yourself is influ-enced by external forces, and as you continue to mature, the meaning you assign to that experience shifts.

This is exactly what happened to me.

As I mentioned back in the first chapter, I got divorced in my twen-ties. This was a pivotal experience in my life. The story I told myself at that time was, "I failed. I failed my family, my faith, and myself. I'm damaged goods. Who could possibly be interested in me now?" I felt as if I had been branded with a scarlet letter: a capital "D" on my forehead signifying *divorced, damaged, danger*—take your pick.

It wasn't until I met the man who is now my husband that the story began to change. He was pleased that I wasn't some starry-eyed young woman in a race to the altar. I'd been up to the mountain already, so to speak, and I wasn't in a hurry to get back there again. Marriage isn't always like a fairytale, as I'd thought, and he valued that about me. He was the first person who helped me realize that I wasn't "damaged," but rather a strong, independent woman who was smarter and more desirable as a result of my previous experience.

Culture and society also play a role in the story you tell yourself, and the meaning you assign to your life experiences. The cultural beliefs and norms of your family or loved ones, and those you look up to, can dramatically influence how your memories are stored.

Here's another example.

Kurt was born in Germany and moved to the United States with his family when he was very young. Every possession the family had was packed into one large trunk. His parents were indentured servants until they could pay off their passage. Kurt was mercilessly teased and tormented at school. Being German wasn't looked on very kindly at that time.

The story Kurt told himself about this experience was this: "Don't let anyone know where you come from. Be like everyone else. Fit in." For a very long time, he was so ashamed of being an immigrant, and of being poor. Society, and external influences around him, heavily influenced the negativity Kurt assigned to this memory.

It wasn't until later in life that Kurt realized where he came from didn't need to be hidden, and he didn't need to be ashamed. Rather he could share and celebrate it. Now, as CEO of a company, he's able to connect with people in a much more powerful way by simply sharing a bit of his past. People gain a deeper appreciation for who Kurt is today once they've learned more about his humble beginnings and his journey to becoming a self-made man.

The meaning you assign to the experiences you have and how your memories are stored dictate how you're shaped as a result. Leaders I've been fortunate enough to work with all shared stories of their lives, loss, failure, even attempted suicide. The stories that the most successful leaders were telling themselves were what enabled them to not only overcome the experiences in their past but harness the learning they gained going through those experiences to help them thrive going forward.

So what stories have you told yourself about your life experiences? Is it possible that you need to reframe the meaning you've assigned to some of your memories?

These are intriguing questions for you to ponder, but not answer. Not quite yet.

The critical thing to recognize is that, on this journey, you have choices to make. Remember, as the screenwriter for the movie of your life, you have the editing power to change any of the stories you've told yourself. If you're not happy with who you are today, you can choose to change the stories you've told yourself and reframe the meaning you've assigned to the memories that have shaped you. You can choose to be defined by your experiences or learn from them and be grateful for who you've become. You can choose to hide behind them, believing you're broken and irreparable, or you can celebrate your blemishes and scars as a vital part of your SWAGGER.

Wait, what did I just say? Yes, you read that correctly: you can celebrate your flaws. Are you ready to get into that?

Let me explain.

Celebrating Your Scars

Have you ever heard of *kintsugi*?

Kintsugi is the Japanese art of repairing broken pottery using gold. Through this process, once broken and useless pottery is given a new lease on life. Disparate pieces are joined, and the cracks are filled with gold, causing them to gleam and shine. These flaws and scars of gold transform the pottery into works of art.

The cracks become a focal point, instead of something to be hidden. Breaking and repairing are viewed as natural parts of an object's history in Japan. When the process of *kintsugi* is undergone, the brilliant gold cracks are celebrated, transforming the previously broken pottery into exquisite and highly valued art. Since no two pieces of pottery ever break in exactly the same way, each new piece that results from *kintsugi* becomes unique, with its own signature look.

Think of yourself as a piece of *kintsugi* pottery. Every experience you have is like a crack that forms, creating part of a signature look. Just like the uniqueness of your fingerprints, no one has exactly the same experiences as you. The scars formed from your life experiences are part of what makes you not only unique, but extraordinary.

Sometimes an experience you have in your life might cause you to shatter into pieces. Regardless of that damage, the key thing to remember is that you can be put back together and become even more spectacular and unique than you were before.

Renovation is typically the process of improving something that's aged or been broken or damaged. It often refers to a structure but can also be defined as making something new or bringing something back to life. Think of this journey as your personal renovation, putting what might be broken or damaged back together, and making something new out of it.

Right now, you might be thinking, "Well that all sounds great in theory, Jennifer, but how exactly am I supposed to get started on this renovation?"

I'm so glad you asked.

To answer this, let's take another look at *kintsugi*. See, it's not just the art of repairing broken pottery, it's also recognized as a philosophy—*kintsugi* well-being. Perhaps one of the most significant concepts in *kintsugi* well-being is what's called *kansha*.

Kansha is the practice of expressing thanks for the good, the bad, and the ugly, so to speak. It's about finding appreciation for both the blessed and the horrible things that have taken place in your life. *Kansha* is the ability to reframe situations in a way that rewires your brain to find at least some good in every experience, no matter how terrible it seems initially.

Sounds familiar, doesn't it? Sounds a bit like gratitude.

Gratitude is the first **G** in SWAGGER, and it's an incredibly important part of the journey because of the power it holds.

Research shows that feelings of gratitude actually improve feelings of happiness, in addition to overall physical and psychological health. People who practice gratitude tend to be less stressed and feel less pain. They have stronger immune systems, more restful sleep, healthier relationships, and experience higher performance, both professionally and academically.

Gratitude can also be known as "thankfulness." It's defined by *Psychology Today* as "the expression of appreciation for what one has. It's a recognition of value independent of monetary worth." Now, the word choice here is intentional. Notice that the definition focuses on appreciating *what you have*. Gratitude isn't about comparing yourself to others or telling yourself that other people have it much worse than you. It is also not about replacing or suppressing negative emotions with positive ones. No, ultimately, gratitude is really about outcome.

"Wait, what?" you ask. Yes. Outcome.

Think of it like this: Outcome is identifying one thing that happened as a result of an experience, that wouldn't have materialized without the experience, that you can be grateful for.

For instance, I'm currently recovering from an injury I sustained over three months ago. The treatment plan wasn't working so we've now turned to more drastic measures. I am in a walking boot up to my knee intended to immobilize my ankle. My daily exercise is now limited to Pilates, upper-body resistance training, and stretching. I can no longer ride my horses, use my Peloton bike, or walk on my treadmill desk, at least for four weeks.

I certainly don't relish being injured. However, anytime either an injury or an illness occurs, it's also a reminder to be grateful for the times when I'm healthy. I cherish and have a greater appreciation for the opportunities I have in the future to do the activities that bring me joy. Therefore, my outlook changes. Instead of looking at exercise or working out as something I *have* to do, I look at it as something I *get* to do. It's something I'm fortunate enough to be able to do. The outcome for me is around reinvigorating the delight and happiness that's found through everyday activities and tasks that I once took for granted. The experience of being injured or sick helps me find it.

Sometimes it takes an experience to open your eyes to something that was already there, but, for whatever reason, you couldn't see. Sometimes an experience can even create something brand new that didn't previously exist. You might be grateful for how an experience helped you grow and develop because now you're able to do something that would never have been possible before.

That's what I mean by gratitude being about outcome. Make sense?

Good, so, back to the original question. How do you create your personal renovation?

You guessed it: by finding and practicing gratitude for your life experiences. Instead of filling the cracks of your pottery with gold, as in *kintsugi*, you fill the cracks your life experiences create with gratitude. Gratitude *is* your gold; it's what transforms you into a work of art that's waiting to be revealed to the world.

With gratitude as your gold, you can proudly let your blemishes shine. You can own your story and allow yourself to be who you choose to be. Instead of something to be hidden or ashamed of, the scars of your life become part of your beauty, your uniqueness, and your SWAGGER.

That sounds amazing, doesn't it?

The best part about this is that this personal renovation is all within your control. You have everything you need to explore, learn from, and find gratitude for your life experiences. No additional resources are required.

You're starting to get a bit more excited about this, aren't you? Good. There are a few more things to cover before you have a go.

For starters, what does this all look like in practice, in real life? Can you truly find gratitude for life experiences that you barely survived and certainly don't wish to relive or be reminded of?

The answer to that is, unequivocally, "yes." Let's explore two stories of people who were able to do just that.

Gratitude amid Extreme Loss: Aileen

Aileen was pregnant with triplets. She'd shared the news with everyone she knew and worked with. Her friends and family were so excited and happy for her and her husband.

Then, the unthinkable happened. She went into labor at only nineteen weeks. A nightmare had begun.

On Friday evening, she lost the first baby, Duncan, but everything seemed to stabilize—or so she thought. On Saturday morning, she lost the two others, Malcolm and Jamie, as well. All three babies were gone. The joy she had felt had vanished and was replaced with shock and anguish. This was so sudden and so unexpected.

Aileen recalls sitting in the kitchen and crying into her cornflakes.

"I don't want this to define my life," she said to herself.

"Fine then. Don't let it," was her own response, as if she were having a conversation with someone else at the kitchen table.

But the grief didn't just go away. Two days later, her body still thought she had babies to take care of and was producing milk.

However, Aileen was determined not to be one of those people who get consumed by grief. She didn't want to feel unable to be around children or other expecting mothers. She knew that if she was going to move forward, she had to make a choice. She had to consciously choose joy in her life.

Somehow, she found a way forward, one day—one step—at a time.

It was a long time before Aileen was ready to try again. But then, finally, it happened. She was pregnant with twins! Fear gripped her at first, overriding the joy she was supposed to be experiencing. She was afraid to share the news with anyone because of what had happened. The thought of it was just too painful.

Would she have to relive the nightmare of her first pregnancy? Would she lose these babies too?

Aileen couldn't even take out the mattress that had been bought for the baby crib. She became so worried that she'd jinx the pregnancy and was unable to truly find any of the joy she had once felt.

Aileen was on bed rest for ten weeks and couldn't leave the house except for doctor appointments. She followed every instruction and precaution to the letter. She did everything in her power to protect and care for herself and the babies during that pregnancy.

Despite these efforts, the nightmare returned.

Aileen couldn't believe this was happening again. It felt like déjà vu.

"What horrible thing have I done to deserve this?" she wailed. "Am I being punished?"

"You know that's not true," she replied to herself. "You don't believe that."

Her thoughts turned over and over in her head.

Could she have done something different? Or better? Could she have gone to another hospital? Would this have happened if she had higher quality care?

"Did I do something wrong?" she even asked the doctor during one of her visits.

"Let me ask you this," he calmly replied. "Did you choose the sex of the children?"

"Well, no, of course not," she answered.

"Exactly," the doctor continued. "That is the amount of control you have over this pregnancy."

Baby Ginny was born with all kinds of issues. Aileen and her husband knew she was not going to be with them very long.

In total, Ginny lived for eleven days. A light in the darkness was that Aileen's mother was able to see Ginny and share some of that time with her daughter and granddaughter. Aileen and the family held a memorial service and laid her remains to rest. Their other baby, Gavan, was still alive, but he too had medical issues, and doctors were unsure if he'd survive.

Miraculously, Gavan is now a teenager.

Through it all, Aileen had to figure out how to navigate being a woman who had lost four babies and was the mother of one. A quote that helped guide her through that time of extreme loss is from Victor Frankl, the author, neurologist, psychiatrist, philosopher, and Holocaust survivor.

"Between stimulus and response," Mr. Frankl said, "there is a space. In that space is our power to choose our response. In our response lies our growth and our freedom."

Aileen realized that she had the power to choose her response to the tragedies in her life. All too often, we don't create that space, and we certainly don't often recognize that we have the power to choose. We simply react and respond in the moment. Then, that response becomes our identity, and who we are going forward.

"I had to consciously choose to let go of the anger and guilt," Aileen remarked. "I had to stop focusing on what I'd lost and instead focus on what I'd gained. I had to choose joy, to recognize all that we had to be grateful for and joyful about.

"Was it easy?" she continued. "No. And I wish I would've realized this sooner that you have the power to choose your response. If you don't like your response, you can change it later."

Aileen decided to choose joy and gratitude over anger and grief. Of course, the pain of what she went through has eased over time, and she has learned to find and create happiness in her life. She reminds herself to find joy every day.

Aileen will never forget what happened, however, she refuses to let her traumatic experiences define who she is today.

Gratitude for a New Normal: Sarah

Sarah's life had just taken off. At only 19, she was accepted into the Under 25 (U25) Equestrian Emerging Athlete Program for the United States—the path to the Olympic team. Her dreams and all that she'd worked for were finally coming true.

However, life had other plans, and unbeknownst to her, Sarah was about to embark on a completely different journey, one she could've never imagined.

Sarah was scheduled to leave for training with the U25 Emerging Equestrian Athletes in Florida on January 10. On January 8, her life and her dreams shattered in an instant. As she and another trainer were turning out the horses for the day, the horse that was being led in front of her broke free and raced backward to kick the horse that Sarah was leading.

The horse did not succeed in kicking the horse Sarah was leading but did make direct contact with Sarah. The kick landed on the right side of her face, splitting her lip up to her nose and breaking almost all the bones on that side.

So, instead of training with the U25 Emerging Equestrian Athletes, Sarah was fighting for her life. In the first of many surgeries to come, the doctors focused on reconstructing and repairing the physical damage done in the accident.

However, there was much more that Sarah was going to have to deal with outside of the physical pain and trauma.

"I've always defined myself through my riding," Sarah remarked. "I've never broken a bone or had to take any time off from riding before. I'm highly competitive, and I like to get things done," she said. "I was in college at the time of my accident. I needed to focus on something other than my injury, so I was back in classes about three weeks following my first surgery."

Due to her competitive spirit and drive, Sarah was determined to get back into the swing of things. She was not only back at school, but she was also back in the saddle. She rode in her first competition only three months after her surgery. Looking back now, Sarah realizes that she went back to everything too soon. She suffered from extreme headaches, likely caused by an undiagnosed concussion, and other complications from not allowing her body the time it needed to heal.

Sarah began a relentless schedule of school, training, competitions, and surgeries. The harder she pushed to get back to her schoolwork and competitive riding, the more toll it took on her body, her mind, and her emotional well-being.

"I went through three surgeries in the first year," she recalls. "Two in the second, and another in the third."

"With each surgery, I felt like I was going backward instead of moving forward," she continued. "I felt as if I was in a vicious cycle of making progress and having it taken away again. It was an incredibly frustrating and emotional time for me."

"I was trying to be so positive through it all, but I was really struggling." Sarah's voice broke. "My mom has always been my rock, and I'll never forget the day she said to me that I wasn't the same person anymore. My mom had voiced what I knew to be true deep down."

"This was a real turning point for me," she said. "I was angry and sad. I not only had to heal from my injuries, which was an excruciating ordeal, to say the least. But I also had to learn to get used to the new me. I was fundamentally changed. I had to come to terms with the fact that I was never going to look the same way again. No matter how hard the surgeons tried, the old me was gone. I had to learn to love the new me and appreciate my new normal instead of wishing I could go back to the way I looked before, and my old life."

Despite ongoing surgeries, Sarah continued with her schooling and competitive riding. She had a plan, and she was determined to see it through. She succeeded in trying out and making it into the U25 US Emerging Equestrian Athlete Program three consecutive years. She graduated with her bachelor of science degree and is currently working on obtaining a global master of business administration degree.

Looking back, Sarah sees her accident and the journey that transpired as one of the best learning experiences of her life.

"I've learned so much through this experience," she says. "There are so many things I know now that I wish I would've known before. This was such a huge challenge for me, and I was only 19 when it happened. You're just not equipped at that age to deal with something of this magnitude."

She continued: "I've learned to appreciate the good things in life and realize that you've no idea what other people have gone through. I've learned to accept change and that I'm stronger than I imagine. I've learned to minimize the noise, focus on what actually matters in life, and let go of what doesn't. I've learned that it's okay to ask for help, that you're not expected to do everything by yourself, and that there are so many people ready to be there for you and support you."

"I wish I knew earlier how important it is to take the time to recover. I set myself back because I pushed myself too much too soon. I wish I would've taken more time to fully recover and get stronger physically, mentally, and emotionally. I know it might sound strange, but I can honestly say that I'm grateful for having gone through this experience. I know that I'm a much better person because of it."

Sarah was fundamentally changed through this experience. She has a deeper appreciation for things she once took for granted. She has more sympathy and compassion for others and what they're going through in life. She's found and pushed past the boundaries of her own strength, and she's acquired wisdom that far exceeds her youth.

Sarah was able to find gratitude for her new normal, to learn to love and appreciate the new version of herself and her life.

Employing the Power of Expressive Writing

Hopefully you see that it's possible to find gratitude for even the most traumatic and dire experiences of your life.

Earlier in this chapter, I mentioned that I've seen firsthand the transformative power of this approach. That's because I've personally experienced the dramatically cathartic impact that exploring your life experiences can provide. I've also witnessed observable changes in the countless leaders I've worked with around the world following the completion of these activities.

So where does this transformative power come from?

To answer this, let's turn to the work of Dr. James Pennebaker, Centennial Liberal Arts Professor of Psychology at the University of Texas at Austin.

Dr. Pennebaker was studying the physiological response of the body to stress when he uncovered something counterintuitive and fascinating: the "confession effect."

When working with top-level polygraphers, Dr. Pennebaker discovered that when being questioned, people often showed intense physiological stress, but once they confessed or shared a secret they'd been holding in, they became extraordinarily relaxed and liberated. Dr. Pennebaker used these findings to focus his research on how expressive writing, instead of sharing secrets out loud, could help people who experienced trauma.

The first of many studies using expressive writing took place in 1986. In this experiment, participants were asked to write for 15 minutes per day for four days. The control group was instructed to write objectively about superficial topics that were provided by the research team. The experimental groups were asked to write about their innermost thoughts, feelings, and emotions surrounding some of the most traumatic events they'd experienced in their lives.

The groups were encouraged not to worry about spelling or grammar and were reassured that all of their writing was confidential. The only rule they were given was to write continuously once they started, and to stop when the time was up.

In this and the many studies that followed, the researchers noticed that many of the participants in the experimental groups became emotional during the writing sessions. They also found that, compared to the control group, the participants who practiced expressive writing made significantly fewer visits to the doctor and experienced numerous physiological benefits, such as decreased anxiety, blood pressure, pain, stress, and depression. They exhibited improvements in their social life, sleep quality, memory, as well as academic and professional performance.

As part of his ongoing research, Dr. Pennebaker studied the differences in the way people used language in their expressive writing. He and his team noticed that people who gained the most benefit from the exercise explored their experiences from multiple perspectives using words like "I," "he," "she," and "they." Additionally, these people also used more cognitive words such as "think," "reason," "consider," or "realize," which demonstrated an ability to identify insights and learn from these experiences to find a productive path forward.

The act of revisiting and writing expressively about your life experiences has well-documented physical, mental, and emotional benefits. The exercises I'm going to ask you to do will enable you to analyze, learn from, and find gratitude for these experiences, as well as help you let go of things you've held on to or kept hidden for far too long.

The release and liberation you feel when you let go of what's been holding you back are profound and create the opportunity for you to move forward positively and productively.

Finding Gratitude for Life Experiences

You're likely getting more excited about this activity and wondering when you'll get the chance to give it a try. Hang in there. It's almost time. I've found through my work with others that it's helpful to provide examples before I ask you to do it yourself.

In these examples, I explore a couple of extremely pivotal moments in my life, sharing the following:

- Why I chose these moments
- What I've learned from them
- The gratitude I've found
- How these moments have helped shape who I am today

The difference between this and what I'll ask you to do is that I'm sharing my experiences and learning with you. You won't be asked to share your experiences with anyone else unless you choose to. That's completely up to you.

Alright then, let's get started.

Moment 1: Severe Test Anxiety

You might have noticed by now that I call myself a "recovering perfectionist." What you probably don't know is where this tendency began, and that's the reason I chose this moment.

It all started one day when I was asked to take a timed multiplication test as a child. I had studied, and I was prepared. However, I panicked when the test started, and I completely blanked. I couldn't even write my own name at the top of the page. My heart raced, and I broke into tears.

From that point on, I developed "severe test anxiety." I would get so worried about an upcoming exam that I would get physically ill and not be able to sleep the night before. To cope with that test anxiety, I would over prepare. I would memorize everything. I could tell you where on the page and what page number a particular piece of information was located.

This moment in my life helped me train my brain to learn and memorize information. I began to use different techniques, like acronyms, to help me remember things. I was eventually able to overcome the physical impact of my test anxiety and continued to strengthen my studying and test preparation techniques throughout high school and college.

The skills I've gained from this experience have helped me succeed in my academic and professional work. I remember getting ready for one of the first presentations I was invited to deliver for a large conference. I spent the whole night before memorizing my presentation and my talking points. It was a good thing too because the next morning as I was getting ready to go onto the stage, there was a technical issue with my computer. Consequently, I had no slides or visuals to back up my presentation. It was just me and the audience. I was so grateful that I'd memorized everything the night before, and it turned out to be a fantastic presentation because I was able to truly connect with the audience instead of hiding behind slides or a podium. This was a great learning moment for me and one that wouldn't have happened had it not been for my test anxiety as a child.

You can imagine how my memorizing and recall techniques came in handy as a global leadership consultant as well. Being able to remember all of the objectives, activities, and learning outcomes while facilitating multiday programs without referring to your notes was a requirement of the job.

Additionally, I was often called on to attend meetings with different clients on the same day. That meant being able to know exactly where we were in a given project or program design, digging into the details, and then having to shift gears and do the same thing with the next client moments later. Having honed my ability to recall and retain information enabled me to navigate this challenging dynamic well.

If it weren't for this experience in my life, and the techniques I employed to overcome it, I wouldn't have become a global leadership consultant at all. I had challenged myself to learn all the names of the women at a party I'd been invited to attend. It was this ability that caught the attention of one woman in particular, who worked for the company that ultimately hired me.

You might not know it at the time, but when you look back at experiences in your life, you connect the dots and recognize how so many things are linked to something that began with just one moment. Even as I'm writing this, I keep coming up with more and more connections for how this experience has helped me in my life.

If it weren't for this experience, you probably wouldn't be reading this book, because the SWAGGER method wouldn't exist. I'm truly grateful for so many things that have transpired as a result of this experience, and I know it has had a massive impact on who I am and how I show up today.

Moment 2: Rest in Peace

In the beginning of the book, you may recall I mentioned the death of my sister. She passed away when she was only in her thirties. She was survived by her husband and two small children. I remember thinking that she would never get a chance to see her children grow up, graduate from school, or experience the lives they would create for themselves. It was so sudden and so sad. I don't think my parents ever got over it. Parents aren't supposed to lose a child, no matter what age they are. It's meant to be the other way around.

This was a pivotal moment in my life for many reasons. Being faced with a loss like this caused me to realize how very precious life is. It forced me to look at things differently and find a greater appreciation for things that I previously took for granted. This moment created a huge mindset shift for me. I stopped complaining about things and started looking for gratitude instead.

I had to deal with a lot of guilt I felt when she passed. I hadn't spoken to her in many months. It wasn't like we were estranged or anything. It just wasn't the nature of our relationship to communicate that often. We were at different places in our lives and weren't all that close. However, that didn't change the fact that her death was permanent; I couldn't just say, "Oh, I'll reach out to her next week." There was no next week. It took a while for me to process this guilt and finally be able to let it go.

As a result of my sister's death, I've developed stronger relationships with my family and friends. Instead of thinking or saying, "I'll call them tomorrow," I call, text, or email whoever it is that I'm thinking about at that moment—right away. I make sure to communicate regularly and not let too much pass without connecting. No more wasting precious time. I've got no idea what tomorrow will bring.

This sentiment has become a cornerstone of my beliefs and my daily life. I often use the phrase, "No day but today." I truly live in the present and cherish every moment as if it might be my last. When so many people complain about getting older, I remind them of one of my favorite sayings: "Do not regret getting older, it is a privilege denied to many." I coach myself around this frequently, especially when my body chooses to remind me of the many wonderful things that transpire as we age—a little sarcasm for you there.

My husband is a saver. He likes to put things away for later use. He still has items he's purchased that have never been worn. I'm the exact opposite. With my "no day but today" approach to life, I like to use things right away. If I've purchased new clothes or shoes, I like to find an opportunity to wear them immediately. If I've come up with a new idea for a recipe, I like to try it out for dinner that night.

Another incredibly important lesson I learned as a result of my sister's passing was the impact and power of vulnerability. However, it was a lesson that didn't become apparent until much later in life.

I was helping my parents and my sister's husband plan the memorial service. We were selecting the songs and hymns to be sung, who would attend, and where she was to be buried.

But there was a piece missing: no one was selected to give the eulogy.

This was my sister. Somebody had to say something about who she was and talk about her life.

So I volunteered.

Now, remember my perfectionist tendencies? Well, they showed up in force. After many hours and many tearful iterations later, I had finally finished her eulogy that I was to deliver at the service. I practiced and practiced and practiced some more. I was absolutely perfect in my practice. However, no matter how much you practice, you can't truly prepare for how you're going to react in reality.

The day of the service came, and I was finding it difficult to hold my emotions in check. I got up to share the eulogy I'd prepared, and I couldn't speak. I was overcome with sadness. Everything that I'd been trying to hold together came undone and flooded to the surface. My mom said that if I'd taken one more minute, she was going to come up and help me down from the pulpit. Whatever the case, it probably only lasted a minute or two, but up there it seemed like an eternity, standing in front of everyone, unable to utter a word.

I finally composed myself and began. I must've known that this was going to happen somehow, because the first sentence of the eulogy asked the audience to be patient with me. Eventually, I was able to make it through the eulogy. When I finally sat back down, I was utterly exhausted and emotionally drained. Following the service, I had so many people come up to me and tell me that it was the best eulogy they'd ever heard.

That moment taught me an incredibly powerful lesson. I'd wanted to be perfect for my sister, for her to be proud of me. I'm an extremely private person and showing emotion in front of others wasn't what I would've considered perfect or professional. I had no idea why people thought I'd done a good job. In my mind, I'd let my sister down.

It wasn't until I was preparing to share the story of my sister's passing for the first time that I truly learned the power of the lesson I was provided that day many years ago.

I was attending a facilitation workshop with several of my peers when I was given one of the best pieces of feedback I'd ever received. We were asked to give each other feedback on something specific we could do to improve our facilitation. I received identical feedback from three different people. These were people I highly respected and admired. They suggested that I needed to demonstrate more vulnerability in front of the room.

This came as a complete shock to me. My perfectionist tendencies didn't leave room for vulnerability. In my mind, I needed to demonstrate strength, expertise, knowledge, and professionalism when facilitating— *not* vulnerability.

However, I took the feedback to heart and vowed to do something about it. I reflected on the experience I had when delivering the eulogy for my sister in preparation for the activity I'd agreed to do the following day.

That's when it hit me. I realized that it wasn't about the perfect words or delivering them perfectly. Perfection at that moment delivering the eulogy was about being human, allowing myself to be vulnerable and not hide my very real emotions. That's what people responded to and what they connected with.

The very next day I shared the story of my sister's death and the experience I had of delivering the eulogy at her service. This was the first time I'd ever shared this story with anyone else, let alone in front of a room full of people.

I managed to control my emotions, but they were extremely visible just under the surface to everyone in attendance. I saw several of my colleagues with tears in their eyes, and that's when I grasped the power of vulnerability and the magnitude of this amazing learning opportunity I was experiencing. I had created a real connection, a human connection, with every single person in that room.

The experiences I've had as a result of my sister's death have enabled me to embrace my vulnerability and generate deeper and more meaningful connections with others. I wouldn't be the facilitator I am today or be here right now sharing this with you if I hadn't lived those experiences.

Do I miss my sister? Yes, every single day. Do I wish I could've done things differently when she was still alive? Absolutely. However, I'm so grateful for the lessons I've learned and how I've grown and developed as a result of the experiences that took place.

Now It's Your Turn

Guess what?

The time has finally come for you to put some of this to work. The following activities provide instructions on how to begin revisiting, learning from, and finding gratitude for your life experiences.

Take a deep breath because this is going to be good.

Please keep in mind that exploring your life experiences can elicit powerful feelings and emotions. Don't worry if you find yourself becoming emotional during these activities. That's completely natural. When you ask your brain to recall experiences that have been hidden away for a while, emotions are bound to resurface. Everyone processes things differently, so just be patient with yourself and don't judge your response.

A Final Important Note

Please keep in mind that exploring your life experiences can elicit powerful memories and emotions. Don't hesitate to seek professional assistance to support your efforts to revisit, learn from, and find gratitude for your life experiences.

Activity: Identifying Your Pivotal Moments
Time: 30 Minutes

The first step in finding gratitude for your life experiences is to identify pivotal moments in your life.

What do I mean by pivotal?

Pivotal moments are those that are of vital or critical importance in your life. They're important because other things depend on them. They're important because, as described in this chapter, they've helped shape who you are and how you show up today.

Step 1
Set aside at least 30 minutes of uninterrupted time to complete this activity. Find a quiet place that's conducive to reflective work and a setting that enables you to record your responses. Make sure you're in a private location so you won't be worried if your emotions rise to the surface.

Step 2
Identify at least four of the most pivotal moments of your life. These can be from any point in time, such as childhood, teenage years, young adulthood, the present day, etc. At least two of these moments should represent stressful, traumatic, or challenging times in your life. Record each moment on a separate piece of paper or a separate page on your computer. Create a name or title for each moment that corresponds with what it's about.

Step 3
Answer the following questions for each moment you've selected.

- Why do you consider this a pivotal moment in your life?
- What story have you told yourself about this moment?
- What meaning have you assigned to this memory?
- How has that story/meaning shaped your behavior?
- What would you like to change about the story/meaning you've assigned to this memory?

Activity: Letting Go
Time: 20 Minutes

This activity is about letting yourself go, letting your thoughts, feelings, and emotions flow freely. It's important to remember that whatever you choose to write is completely confidential. These activities are for you and your SWAGGER journey. If you choose to share your work with anyone else as part of your journey, that's completely up to you.

Step 1
Find a quiet place that's conducive to reflective work and a setting that enables you to write without interruptions. Make sure you're in a private location so you won't be worried if your emotions rise to the surface.

Step 2
Select one of the pivotal moments you identified in the previous activity to focus on. This should be a moment that reflects one of the most traumatic and challenging times in your life.

For ten minutes, write continuously about your deepest thoughts, feelings, and emotions related to this experience. You can write about anything that comes to mind related to this experience. There is no wrong way to do this. You can write about who else was involved, how you felt, what happened, why it was so traumatic, whatever direction your thoughts take you.

Don't worry about spelling or grammar, just write. Let your thoughts flow freely.

Step 3
Identify one thing that has happened in your life as a result of this experience that you're grateful for. This is something that wouldn't have taken place without you having experienced this challenging and traumatic moment. Record your thoughts, specifically highlighting what it is that you're grateful for.

Daily Reinforcement: Finding Gratitude
Time: 5 Minutes

The more you practice finding gratitude, the easier it'll be to see. This daily reinforcement encourages you to find gratitude for the everyday things that exist in your life.

Step 1
Find a quiet place to sit down. Close your eyes and listen to your breath. On the inhale, say quietly to yourself, "Inhale." On the exhale, say quietly to yourself, "Exhale." Do this for one minute to clear and calm your mind.

Step 2
Think of at least one thing you have to be grateful for right now. It could be a person, a roof over your head, your ability to walk or see, food to eat, etc. Capture all of the thoughts that come to mind using this to begin each statement: *"I'm grateful for . . ."*

Step 3
Say your gratitude statements out loud several times or until you begin to feel a shift in your mindset and attitude. Use this technique whenever you find yourself overcome with stress or negativity. You can also use this technique first thing in the morning when you wake up to set the tone for your day.

Daily Reinforcement: Gratitude for Others
Time: 5 Minutes

The practice of finding gratitude doesn't just involve being grateful for the things in your life. It's also about the people you engage with. This daily reinforcement focuses on finding gratitude for someone who's had an impact on you in your life.

Step 1

Identify a person in your life for whom you're grateful. Select someone who is still alive (you'll understand why in the next step). Make a list of all the reasons why you're grateful for this individual.

Step 2

Call or send a written note to thank this person for being in your life. Make sure to highlight the many reasons why you're grateful for them.

 ## SWAGGER Insight

- Finding gratitude for the life you have doesn't require going back in time.
- You're a product of your past.
- Everything I've experienced in my past has made me who I am today.
- While there are times to reflect on, learn from, and perhaps even share your past, there are also other times where you just have to let the past go.
- Your life experiences have an enormous impact on shaping how you show up in your life today, and who you choose to be.
- Think of your brain as a vast filing system that categorizes and files away every experience you have from the time you're born.
- With every experience categorized, your brain also logs information about the situation, who or what was involved, how you felt, the emotions elicited, and the meaning you assigned to it.
- There's a direct connection between how the brain records and categorizes experiences and the subsequent elicited behavior.
- Your brain works to help you make sense of and figure out how to engage with the world around you.
- Your brain's vast catalog of past experiences holds the keys to why you behave the way you do *today*.
- Your past experiences form the framework for who you are and

who you will become.

- Your brain automatically categorizes new information based on your previous experiences.
- Your brain uses neural pathways to communicate information and create behavioral responses.
- Over time, your brain strengthens and works to optimize the most commonly used neural pathways, and the stronger a pathway becomes, the more ingrained the resulting pattern of behavior is.
- The good news is that this process enables you to create deep subject-matter expertise. The challenging news is, as your brain matures, its heavily used neural pathways become more and more entrenched, which makes the corresponding patterns of behavior to those pathways that much more defined, and therefore, harder to break free from and change.
- Your brain follows the path of least resistance.
- You can learn and create new behaviors at any age.
- Learning new things becomes harder as you get older and your neural pathways begin to solidify. Your brain loses flexibility and plasticity as you age.
- The pathways that begin to form in your brain in your youth tend to stay with you and shape your behavior for a long time.
- How you view your life experiences, and the stories you tell yourself about them, become increasingly significant to who you are now. The stories you tell yourself directly impact your current mindset, confidence, and self-worth. These stories shape your behaviors, choices, and actions.
- The stories you tell yourself can be influenced by external forces, and the meaning you assign to those experiences can shift as you mature over time.
- The cultural beliefs and norms of your family or loved ones, and those you look up to, can dramatically influence how your memories are stored.
- You are the screenwriter for the movie of your life and have the

editing power to change any of the stories you've told yourself. If you're not happy with who you are today, you can choose to change the stories you've told yourself and reframe the meaning you've assigned to the memories that have shaped you.

- You can choose to be defined by your experiences or learn from them and be grateful for who you've become. You can choose to hide behind them, believing you're broken and irreparable, or you can celebrate your blemishes and scars as a vital part of your SWAGGER.

- Like in *kintsugi* pottery, every experience you have is like a crack that forms, creating part of your signature look. Regardless of the damage your life experiences cause, the key thing to remember is that you can be put back together and become even more spectacular and unique than you were before.

- In *kintsugi* well-being, *kansha* is the ability to reframe situations in a way that rewires the brain to find at least some good in every experience, no matter how terrible it initially seems.

- Gratitude holds immense power to improve happiness, health, relationships, and performance.

- Gratitude is about focusing on *what you have*. Gratitude isn't about comparing yourself to others or telling yourself that other people have it much worse than you. It's also not about replacing or suppressing negative emotions with positive ones.

- Gratitude is about outcome; identifying one thing that happened as a result of an experience that you can be grateful for that wouldn't have materialized without the experience.

- Instead of filling the cracks of your pottery with gold, as in *kintsugi*, you fill the cracks your life experiences create with gratitude. Gratitude *is* your gold; it's what transforms you into a work of art that's waiting to be revealed to the world.

- With gratitude as your gold, you can proudly let your blemishes shine. You can own your story and allow yourself to be who you choose to be. Instead of something to be hidden or ashamed of, the scars of your life become part of your beauty, your uniqueness, and your SWAGGER.

- You have everything you need to explore, learn from, and find gratitude for your life experiences.
- Using expressive writing to explore your life experiences can help you analyze, learn from, and find gratitude for, as well as let go of, things you've kept hidden for far too long.
- The release and liberation you feel when you let go of what's been holding you back are profound and create the opportunity for you to positively and productively move forward.

CHAPTER 6

Becoming Grounded in Your Core Values

Have you ever wondered why palm trees don't fall over in a storm? Whether it's a hurricane, a monsoon, or a tropical storm, when the wind calms, palm trees are almost always still standing when everything else around them has been destroyed.

Why is that?

It turns out that the way palm trees are designed has a lot to do with their ability to hold fast in a storm. They have large root structures made up of hundreds of "spaghetti" roots that form what's called a root ball. This root ball can be anywhere from one to five feet long, depending on the maturity of the tree.

In addition, palm trees are incredibly elastic. They have fibrous trunks that contain a high moisture content, which enables them to bend readily under pressure instead of breaking. They also have a smaller top profile than many other trees. When compared with larger canopies, palm trees create much less resistance, so the wind cuts through their leaves with ease.

So what, exactly, does this have to do with core values?

Well, I'd like you to think of your own core values as your root ball. The more you nurture and live your values, the larger and stronger your root ball will become, making it easier to withstand the storms that life throws at you. When you're firmly anchored and grounded in your core values, just like a palm tree, you're not easily swayed or blown over. You can stand firm and tall against even the fiercest winds.

See, it's your core values that create a foundation for your SWAG-GER. They form an anchor that enables your SWAGGER to thrive. Simply put, without your core values, your SWAGGER can't exist. Therefore, in order to claim your SWAGGER, you have to identify what your core values are, understand why they're important to you, and determine how to live them daily.

Now, I know what you're probably thinking right now . . .

"Wait, what? I've gotten this far in my SWAGGER journey, and now you're saying my SWAGGER can't exist without core values. How do I know what my core values are?"

Don't worry. You already have core values—most people do, whether they know it or not. The thing is, your values might just be hidden away for safekeeping, so they aren't readily accessible to you right at this moment, or on the tip of your tongue.

What a relief, right? Okay, well, now it's time for you to take them out of that special box you keep them in and bring them out into the light.

Back in Chapter 2, I encouraged you to think of this journey of self-discovery as your personal treasure hunt. This chapter is intended to help you identify and become grounded in your core values so you can live them daily. So think of this chapter as a puzzle you need to solve to claim your treasure—your SWAGGER.

Excited? Great! Then let's start by gaining a better understanding of what core values are.

Demystifying Values

Over the years, I've worked with many organizations, each with their own set of values. You've likely seen such values on company websites or highlighted in corporate communications. They typically involve short hot-button phrases meant to encapsulate an ethos—phrases like "customer focus," "transparency," "be the change you seek," "move fast," etc.

But what do core values actually tell you about a company?

Essentially, an organization's core values tell you who they are and how they behave. They're the internal beliefs and guiding morals that shape the actions and decisions of the employees, and the company as a whole. Organizational values dictate how it conducts itself when working to achieve objectives, deliver on a strategy, and accomplish a vision.

Okay, then, so what about *personal* core values?

Well, first of all, picture an iceberg. Got that visual? Fantastic.

Now, icebergs can be quite deceptive. What you see on the surface only tells part of the story. There's often a large portion of the iceberg hidden beneath the surface.

So think of yourself as this iceberg. What sits above the water line are your decisions, actions, and behaviors. These are what's visible to other people and how you engage with the world around you. But what sits beneath the surface, what people don't see, are the things that shape what shows up above the water line. These are your strengths, life experiences, and values that influence your decisions, actions, and behaviors.

We've already focused on your strengths and life experiences in past chapters, but we haven't yet discussed your values.

Your core values are intimately connected to your needs and what you deem as important in your life. Because they're directly linked to what's important to you, they're the most powerful motivators for personal action. Similar to an organization, your core values play a vital role as your internal compass, which guides your decisions and actions.

For example, let's say two of your core values are "development" and "appreciation," and you're in the process of deciding whether or not to take a new position within the company you work for. This position will involve reporting to a new manager. Given that you highly value development and appreciation, you take time to interview others who are currently working with or have worked with this manager. You ask questions to uncover how this manager helped develop people on the team and whether or not people felt appreciated.

See the connection?

You don't just make a decision based on a "gut feeling." Rather, you use your core values to guide you in making an informed decision, one that aligns with those values.

Roy E. Disney, nephew of Walt and longtime Walt Disney executive said, "When your values are clear, making decisions becomes easier."

Your core values are fundamental to who you are and how you engage with the world. They shine a light on what's critically important to you at a particular time in your life. They're influenced by many aspects, such as experiences, education, religion, or culture. Your core values can evolve over time, based on whatever stage of life you're in.

If you're just starting your career, for instance, you might value "advancement" and "prosperity." If you're someone getting ready to retire, your values might include "family," "freedom," and "fun." If you've survived a serious illness like cancer, you might highly value "well-being" and "gratitude." If you've served in the military, perhaps your values include "loyalty," "order," and "service."

These are just a few examples of how your core values can shift and change based on your experiences and where you are in your life.

Most importantly, your core values are personal, and therefore unique to you.

For example, let's say you list "pleasure" and "fun" in your top five core values. That means you focus on enjoying the process of completing your work and having fun along the way. Your exacting boss, on the other hand, might value "achievement" and "excellence." So while you're focused on having fun, your boss is stressed about achieving goals and making sure final products meet high standards of excellence.

Get the idea? Two people. Very different sets of values.

Missing in Action

As previously stated, your core values play a vital role in your internal compass, the guide for your actions and decisions.

But, as I alluded to earlier, what happens if your core values are hidden away for safekeeping? How do they guide your actions if they're not readily accessible?

To answer this, let's explore a couple scenarios and the corresponding impact of values that are missing in action.

Scenario 1

Amit has been asked to lead a task force aimed at streamlining how "go" or "no-go" decisions are made for future projects. He's excited about leading this initiative because he recognizes the impact this could have on his standing and reputation within the company. He understands that taking on this assignment will require longer hours and additional work on top of what he's doing in his current role. However, he feels that the upside potential of leading this task force will outweigh the extra effort and time he'll need to put in.

Amit decides to accept the assignment and begins work immediately with eagerness and enthusiasm.

Weeks into the initiative, the longer hours and added work begin to take a toll. Amit finds himself becoming more and more stressed. He's consistently coming home late from work, and he recently missed his son's piano recital, which he was so looking forward to attending. His enthusiasm for this task force has waned, and the quality of his performance in all areas has begun to suffer.

He was so excited about taking on this assignment, so how did Amit get to this point?

As it turns out, three of Amit's core values are "advancement," "family," and "quality." He thought he'd weighed the pros and cons of taking the lead on the task force, but what he neglected to do was consider his core values. They were missing in action when his decision was made.

Amit is stressed and unhappy because his professional decision put his core values at odds with one another. His desire for advancement tipped the scales and encouraged him to take the assignment. However, in doing so, he let his family down, missing out on family dinners and attending his son's recital.

This all created a huge internal conflict in Amit that, without being identified or addressed, would only continue to get worse. Because he was so unhappy, even the time he did spend with his family was strained. He found himself lacking the patience he normally had, lashing out, and overreacting to everything. Additionally, Amit prides himself on always delivering exceptional quality in his work. When his workload increased due to the new role on the task force, he was no longer able to perform and deliver at the same level of quality. This caused significant frustration and anxiety. He began to doubt his abilities, which only deteriorated his performance further.

Now, I'm not saying that Amit would've made a different decision if he'd considered his values. What I am saying is, if he still chose to lead the task force, there are several things he could've done to align with his core values instead of putting them at odds with one another. For example, he could've discussed off-loading some current responsibilities with his boss so he could take on the extra work without stretching himself too thin. He could've had conversations with his family in advance so that they were on board with the decision, making them aware of the long hours and events he might miss in the short-term.

If Amit had used his values to help guide him when making the decision, he could've set himself up for success instead of frustration, anger, and self-doubt.

Scenario 2

Gisela just broke up with her latest partner. This has become quite the pattern with her, and she's beginning to feel like she's never going to find someone she can be with long-term. She wonders aloud, "Why does this keep happening to me?"

Gisela's relationships begin the same way every time. She meets someone, and there's an instant connection. They agree to meet for coffee, and they realize that they have so much in common. One thing leads to another, and before you know it, they're "seeing" each other.

Gisela has a high-powered job and is extremely focused on her career, so she often works long hours and travels frequently. She's also training for a triathlon, which takes up a significant amount of her time outside of work.

The dynamic this creates within Gisela is that she feels like she's constantly being asked to choose between her relationship, work, or training. She's torn between multiple priorities, which causes her stress levels to increase and negatively impacts her work and performance. Gisela begins to resent the fact that she's no longer able to find joy in her job or other activities she used to love so much. She's overwhelmed by guilt and stress.

So, like clockwork, Gisela gets to a certain point in the relationship and breaks it off.

"This just isn't working," she claims. "You deserve more than I can give you."

Following the breakup, Gisela is always filled with sadness at first, then relief starts to set in. Over time, she begins to feel like herself again, and all is well, until the cycle repeats itself once more.

What do you think is happening here? Why is Gisela having such a hard time with relationships?

Part of the problem for Gisela is that she's not honoring her values within these relationships. It's clear that Gisela highly values "intimacy" and "stability," and that's what she's seeking in a relationship. She enjoys developing a level of intimacy with her partner and yearns for the stability of a long-term relationship. However, challenges arise when the relationship begins to conflict with her other values: "achievement," "competition," and "freedom." Gisela thrives on accomplishing and achieving her goals both at work and in her athletic endeavors. She gets such a rush from competing and consistently seeks out new opportunities to compete against both herself and others.

Above all, Gisela values freedom. To perform at her best, she needs the freedom to do whatever is required to succeed. That might mean spending extra time at work, logging more miles in training, or taking a recovery day to heal. Her performance significantly suffers when her freedom is stifled, and she feels boxed in or trapped.

What do you think Gisela could do differently going forward to set herself up for success in relationships instead of repeating the same pattern?

Exactly. She can begin by honoring her values.

Now, I'm not saying that values are the only thing at play here, or the only reason Gisela is having difficulty finding that long-term relationship she seeks. However, focusing on honoring her values would be a great place to start, and there are a few things she could do to create a better chance of success.

One of the things Gisela can do is clearly articulate what living her values looks like for her. The more specific she can be, the easier it is to identify and communicate what's lacking or what needs to change. Additionally, she can share her values with her partner her values and what's truly important for her happiness and ability to perform at her best.

So often people fall for someone because of who they are, then spend the entire relationship working to change them into someone else entirely. This is a recipe for disaster, unhappiness, and disappointment.

But when you take the time to share and explain your values to one another, you set clear expectations for what you need from another in a relationship. This will deepen your level of communication and understanding and create a much more productive path forward.

Of course, this can't be done if your values are hidden away for safekeeping.

When you make decisions while your core values are missing in action, frustration, anger, guilt, stress, and other negative responses await you. Just like when you're driving an unfamiliar road and come across a sign that says "Caution, Rough Road Ahead," when you neglect to utilize your values to guide you in your daily life, you're setting yourself up for a bumpy ride.

It doesn't matter what stage of life you're in, or how different your core values are from others. Your core values are like muscles; they function best when exercised regularly. The more you use them, the stronger they become and the more guidance they provide. Conversely, just like muscles, your core values can weaken and atrophy from lack of use.

Another way to look at it would be to think of your core values as an app on your phone.

The apps that you use most often become the easiest to access. Your core values should be the same. When you consistently use your core values to guide your daily actions and help you make decisions, you strengthen the neural pathways that make them easier to access. This is similar to the algorithm on your phone that puts the apps you use most at your fingertips.

So the more you intentionally use your core values, the more they become part of your everyday life. They'll no longer be hidden away like an obscure app you downloaded once and never used again. Your core values will be readily accessible whenever you need additional guidance.

Core Values, Beliefs, & Principles: What's the Difference?

It's quite possible that when you begin to explore your core values, other concepts like "beliefs" and "principles" will start to surface.

Now, what the heck's the difference, and how are they all connected?

Let's start with **beliefs**. Beliefs are assumptions; things you hold to be true. These may or may not exist as a result of any proof, you simply believe them. You use beliefs to help you navigate the world around you. They're often passed down from generation to generation. You form these beliefs over time and through your experiences. Think of beliefs in terms of culture, religion, and politics.

Let's say you were brought up in a Christian family. Based on the teachings you learned in Sunday school, your church, and within your family, you believe that there's one God whose Son died for you and was resurrected for your sins. Or perhaps you were raised in a family that practiced Hinduism, and you believe that all living creatures have a soul. You might've been raised in a culture that believes everything should be done for the good of the community instead of self. Maybe your family instilled in you the belief that you should always respect your elders. Alternatively, you could've been brought up to believe that the government is out to get you and can't ever be trusted. The beliefs you hold today have been heavily influenced by your family, your society and culture, and your experiences.

But how do these beliefs connect to your values?

Your beliefs, the assumptions you hold to be true, create the foundation upon which your values are formed.

For example, based on life experiences, Rafael believes that success can only come from hard work and dedication. Because of this belief, two of his core values are "perseverance" and "discipline." If he has the discipline to work hard enough, he will eventually succeed. See the link between his belief and what he values?

Or take Hannah, who believes life is short and time is limited. This belief she's formed over time has significantly influenced two of the things she values most: "adventure" and "pleasure." She aims to make life a grand adventure and consistently strives to find and create joy in every experience. Notice how her values are shaped by her belief?

So what about **principles**? Where do they fit in? Well, principles tend to be less subjective and more unyielding, often employing qualitative words like "always" and "never." Principles help you distinguish between right and wrong, thus guiding your behavior. Examples of principles might be maxims like "always telling the truth" or "never cheat" or "always take responsibility for your actions" or "never have cause for regret."

Now, of course your values inform your principles. In fact, each value has a corresponding principle that directly impacts how you behave.

For example, if you value "honesty," then a principle that directs your behavior might be never telling a lie, even when the truth is difficult to hear.

See the connection? Let's look at a couple more examples.

"Conservation" is a core value of Kim's. She lives by the principle that she should take care of the environment at all times. Because of this, she recycles, takes public transportation, and carries a reusable water bottle with her wherever she goes.

Arturo highly values "balance." Work-life balance is a principle that shapes his daily life. He religiously makes time for his workouts. He cherishes his evenings making dinner with his wife. Also, he always disconnects from work when he and his family are on vacation.

See how they work together?

Okay, now you give it a go. Match each of the following values with a corresponding principle.

Value	Principle
Fairness	I always seek to find agreement and a peaceful solution.
Reliability	I will always do what is right.
Harmony	I equally apply laws and rules to everyone.
Integrity	I always follow through on what I say I will do.

So how did you do? Are you really starting to get the hang of this, or what?

By using logic and the process of elimination, you can easily connect the dots. It makes perfect sense that "reliability" is connected to following through on what you say you'll do. Seeking to find agreement and a peaceful solution seems to fit well with "harmony." Always doing what is right is best linked with "integrity." That leaves "fairness," which most closely aligns with applying laws and rules equally to everyone.

See, you've got this! Now let's put this all together. Your **beliefs** are the assumptions that help you navigate the world around you and aid in shaping your **values**. Your **values** define what's important to you and inform your **principles**. Your **principles** are the rules that govern your *behavior*.

Beliefs → *shape your* → **Values** → *inform your* →
Principles → *govern your* → **Behavior**

See how they all fit? Isn't it fantastic? So, given this, what happens to your behavior when someone violates your values?

Seeing the Light

A couple quick questions:

Have you ever been waiting in a line, only to watch in horror as someone walks to the front as if the line itself didn't exist and they were more important than everyone else who'd been standing there waiting? Does it drive you crazy when people show up late? How do you react when someone cuts you off in traffic?

If you're anything like me, these seemingly "minor" transgressions can cause intense fury and frustration—and that's probably putting it mildly.

Chances are good that your core values are the "why" behind this resulting hurt and anger. The reality is, when these transgressions take place before your eyes, your core values of "fairness" and "respect" have been wounded and bruised.

When you recognize that your injured values are at the heart of many of your emotional responses, you gain a deeper understanding of what causes your seemingly unusual behavior. Applying new knowledge about your core values to your life can help you identify potential pitfalls and better navigate the world going forward.

Let's explore this further through some examples.

I was up bright and early one morning for a meeting with Sven, a team member of mine from Sweden. At six in the morning my time, with coffee in hand, I began walking on my treadmill desk. I logged into the Zoom meeting and walked while I waited for Sven to join. I walked and waited, losing my patience with each moment that passed. At 6:10, I emailed him. His response: "I am traveling to another client meeting and forgot to tell you that our meeting needed to be changed."

Let me just say this, I was incensed. I couldn't even respond to the email. He tried calling and I didn't pick up. My fury rose, and my thoughts spiraled out of control.

If he's traveling to a client meeting, that means it was probably planned well in advance, and he should've had plenty of time to let me know that our meeting needed to be rescheduled. How rude! He's not the only one who's busy! Does he even care that I had to get up extra early for our meeting today?

I couldn't believe how pissed off I was.

I thought to myself, *Why am I so upset? This is a minor incident, no big deal. So why am I furious? Am I blowing this completely out of proportion?*

After taking a few deep breaths and reflecting on the situation, I figured out why I was so angry. "Respect" is one of my most important core values, and this colleague of mine had completely violated it. Deep down, I know he didn't intentionally try to upset me. Regardless of this fact, I was still irritated and hurt.

Sven and I were leading a high-profile project, the success of which required us to work well together. I knew we needed to resolve this issue for the good of the client and the good of the project. So at our next face-to-face meeting, we took the time to clear the air and shared our core values with each other. I explained why I got so upset about the meeting he neglected to reschedule, and he highlighted something I'd done previously that had frustrated him. Gaining an understanding of what was important to each other helped to foster a deeper trust between us, and significantly improved our working relationship.

Let's look at another example.

I was on a video call with Corinne the other day when the subject of values came up.

"Values are the most powerful predictors of personal action," I said.

Corinne thought about it for a moment, and all of a sudden, her face transformed. She was clearly having one of those "aha" moments. It was as if she'd found the missing piece of a puzzle and everything had come together.

"Wow! That makes so much sense now," Corinne said. "When I'm at my daughter's house and getting ready to leave, she'll often say, 'Please close the door on your way out.' I find myself feeling insulted and hurt when she says this, but never understood why."

"So what do you think now?" I asked, curious to see what she'd learned from her lightbulb moment.

Corinne continued to explain: "One of my values is 'helpfulness,'" she said. "I work to be thoughtful and helpful in all I do. So of course I'm going to close the door! Doesn't she know this about me? Doesn't she trust me to do that? I know it seems like such a small thing to get upset about, but I do, and now I know why. My daughter has discounted one of my core values. Wow! This information is so useful! Thanks for the therapy," she teased.

What do you think: now that Corinne has this new knowledge and understanding, what can she do going forward to remedy this situation?

Similar to my scenario with Sven, a great place to start would be sharing her core values with her daughter. In doing so, Corinne could explain why it upsets her when she's asked to close the door on her way out. Additionally, Corinne might ask what her daughter's core values are and seek to uncover the reason behind her request to close the door.

Sometimes we have to slow down to go fast. By pausing and inquiring, instead of reacting, we can create a learning opportunity.

When you recognize what sits beneath a particular behavior, you reduce the tendency toward anger and frustration and no longer take things as an attack on you personally. You can relax the fight or flight response in your brain, enabling you to assess the situation less emotionally and choose a more productive response.

When you realize that it's your core values that are at the heart of many of these painful experiences, it will truly be one of those "aha" moments for you as well. It's not just a light bulb going on, but an entire city illuminating the night sky. Why? Because you recognize that you're not crazy, just randomly flying off the handle at the slightest mishap. No, you're a rational person, with actions and behaviors deeply rooted in your core values. More importantly, you've stepped into the driver's seat and taken back control. When you become aware of what causes you to get upset, hurt, or angry, you create options. You can choose how you'd like to respond when faced with the same situations in the future. You're no longer simply a slave to your reactionary fight or flight response.

Pretty amazing, isn't it? When you fully embrace and apply this concept, it's a truly liberating experience.

Problems like the scenarios I've illustrated above usually arise when you've neglected to share your core values with those around you. You might assume that everyone knows what your values are and, more importantly, that they share those same values. This is where the disconnect occurs. The reality is most people don't intentionally violate your values. How can they if they don't even know what your values are?

These situations are compounded by the fact that those around you are working off their own set of values that are equally unknown to you. (You can see where this is all going, right?) Making assumptions about values gets you nowhere and sends you directly into a never-ending spiral of unnecessary anger, frustration, and hurt.

Think of your values as a patch of newly planted grass just coming up, still fragile and in need of protection. You assume that every passerby can see that the grass is delicate and will stay off it. A person walking by proceeds to take a shortcut across the grass and tramples all over it. But they didn't willingly disregard your desire for people to stay off the grass. There was no visible sign or any declaration of your request.

Unless your core values are shared and communicated, people can't possibly know what they are. Consequently, you continue to be at risk of having your core values damaged.

It's all starting to make more sense, isn't it?

Courageous Steps

You now hopefully have a better understanding of what core values are, what happens when they're missing in action, how they're connected to your beliefs and principles, and what it looks like when those values are violated.

However, as I've said before, knowing isn't the same as doing. Just knowing what your core values are isn't enough. You have to live them.

Daily. One of the greatest German literary figures of the modern era, Johann Wolfgang von Goethe, said it like this: "Knowing is not enough; we must apply. Willing is not enough; we must do."

So what's it like to truly live your values?

Well, one thing I know for certain is, it takes courage and lots of it. Ever had that horrible recurring dream where you find yourself stark naked in front of a huge audience or a room full of people?

Yeah. It's going to feel a little bit like that.

Living your values takes both courage and a willingness to be bold. You're like a streaker, opening your coat and revealing to the world something intensely personal and meaningful to you. Living your values is just the same as walking out into the world naked. You have to be willing to stand up and say, "Yes, this is what's important to me. I'm living my values regardless of whether or not they're popular or you agree. They're not just words that exist on a wall or in a book, they're alive in my daily decisions and actions."

It's not easy to take out things that are so personal and share them, to allow them and yourself to be vulnerable to being trampled and bruised, to get hurt. You're putting yourself out there, stepping into the arena and allowing yourself to be seen. This is beyond difficult. It's much easier to keep your values hidden away. It's scary to bring them out into the open and lay them on the line.

Given all of this, you might be wondering right now if it's all worth it. I mean why should you go through all the angst and potential hurt—is it worth what you'll get in return?

Listen, I never said this was going to be easy. But I can tell you that this is so very much worth it. Remember, when you nurture and live your values, like the palm trees, you're strengthening that root ball of yours, and you become stronger and more able to withstand any wind you come up against.

When you put on that battle armor, or that superhero cape, and get past the initial fear, when you're daring enough to live your values, you're going to feel a hundred feet tall and bulletproof.

Because see, when you're willing to live your values, you're telling yourself that you matter; that what you *value* matters. It's like a shot of adrenaline for your self-worth, and a booster shot for your SWAGGER. It's a sensation that's hard to explain, but once you feel it, you will definitely want to feel it again.

Perhaps now you're thinking, "But if I've never lived my values before, how will I know when I'm doing it?"

When you're about to do something that scares you, it's a pretty good indication that you're getting ready to put yourself in a vulnerable position and live your values. No, I don't mean the fear you might feel if you were getting ready to jump out of an airplane or zipline through a rainforest.

Now, I'm talking about the fear that arises from doing something or saying something that worries you, that you prepare for, that you suffer sleepless nights over. The fear that makes you question whether or not it's the right thing to do, and you have no idea how what you're going to do or say will be received.

Here, let me see if I can show you what I mean with some real-life examples.

I was facilitating workshops at a leadership conference for a multinational pharmaceutical company.

We were in the plenary session, and the CEO of the company was sharing some of the most significant leadership moments of his life in front of about 400 people. He talked about how the company had recently created a life-changing vaccine. He was so proud of this achievement and the massive impact it could have. The problem was the people who needed this vaccine the most couldn't afford it. So that same CEO decided to produce and supply the vaccine at no profit to the company.

During that day's Q&A session, one of the leaders in the conference asked the CEO what his Board of Directors at the company had thought about his decision.

This is how he replied: "I didn't tell them. It was the right thing to do."

That is what living your values looks like.

Now, I wasn't there with the CEO when he was contemplating this potentially career-altering decision. But I'm certain that he thought long and hard before he made it. He worried about how it would be received. He wondered if he'd lose his job. He tossed and turned through the nights, pondering how it could impact the overall financials of the company. But, in the end, he did it anyway. He was bold and courageous. He stood up for his value of "integrity." He did the right thing, even when it wasn't necessarily popular or in service to himself or his career.

Here's another example.

You might recall from Chapter 1 that I got divorced when I was in my twenties. What I didn't tell you were some of the things that happened leading up to that divorce.

Do you know what it's like to come home from work to find an eviction notice on your front door?

Well, I do. It's gut-wrenching, and not something I'd ever wish on anyone.

I'm not here to complain or blame anyone else. After all, I was part of that relationship. Sure, I naively believed my husband (at that time) when he said he would take care of the bills, and I, to this day, don't know where that money went and why the rent never got paid. However, I also had a part to play in the situation, and I didn't ask any questions when I obviously should have and blindly believed that everything was fine.

I'm only sharing this with you to create some context for a moment that happened much later.

After surviving an experience, during which my whole life was turned upside down and I woke up one morning to find everything I had was gone, I knew I never wanted to be in that situation ever again. I never wanted to feel the panic of frantically trying to figure out a temporary solution for where to live, or hope I had enough money in the account to put gas in my car to get there. I never wanted to wonder if I would come home from work to find another eviction notice on the door for everyone to see. No, this was going to be a one-night-only performance, and I was committed to doing everything in my power to make sure it wouldn't take place ever again in my future.

It's pretty fair to say that this moment in my life shifted my values dramatically. "Security," "stability," "honesty," and "openness" had jumped to the front of the queue for core values. Values reflect what's most important to us at given points in our lives. Well, in an instant, these values had become four of my top five. Funny how that happens.

Now fast-forward in time, and my current husband and I were just starting to see each other. It was no big deal, nothing out of the ordinary, except for the fact that we worked together, and he was my boss . . .

Plot twist, I know.

But where was I supposed to meet anyone when all I did was work? Which, by the way, was exactly what I was doing. I worked extremely long hours, weekends, holidays, you name it. I was always working. He and I saw each other in various professionally pressurized situations: good times, hard times, chaotic times, even dealing with tight deadlines and no sleep. It's actually a great way to get to know someone and learn how they react in times of stress. Through all of this, we became friends. We ran, worked out, and played golf together. We thoroughly enjoyed each other's company. Then one day, it was like a switch flipped and we started to look at each other in a new light. Perhaps, we thought, there was something more there than friendship.

Well, you can imagine how my values of security, stability, honesty, and openness went on high alert. I wasn't going to jeopardize my job or myself for a relationship, no way. I was going to ensure that I could take care of myself and had to put my concerns out there. I had developed a fantastic reputation in the company for being a hard worker who delivered exceptional results. I had a career path mapped out to continue to progress through the ranks. Between the two of us, I had much more to risk if I continued with the relationship.

So I was determined to find out what his intentions were and share my concerns.

To say that I agonized over this is an understatement. I had no idea how he would react or respond. I wrote in a journal exactly what I was going to say to him, and yes, I committed it to memory. My past test anxiety coping mechanisms came in handy.

The moment came when we were walking back to his apartment after working out at the gym. I took a deep breath and steadied myself, then I began.

Believe it or not, I found the exact journal, and the entry, where I wrote the following words all those years ago:

I admire and respect you greatly. I respect who you are, your position, and what you've accomplished. This combination is perfect in the work environment. I love working for you.

However, on the personal side, this same admiration and respect have allowed me to move too quickly and put myself in a very vulnerable position without clarification of the situation.

I've acted in a manner that's completely out of character for me. I've learned that only I can take care of me. I've learned that honesty and openness are essential in all dealings with people. If intentions and expectations are on the table from the beginning, then no one can get hurt or misunderstood.

With that being said, I'd like to know, what are your intentions or expectations for this relationship?

So this is exactly what it looks like to stand up for your values. This was an incredibly scary moment for me that took an enormous amount of courage. But once the words came out, it felt amazing.

Now, maybe you're thinking, "Was that really such a big deal?" Well, for me, it was. It was the first time in my life that I'd shared out loud what was going on inside my head. I'd never before shared my concerns so openly or stood up for what I valued. I'd just given my self-worth a huge shot of adrenaline, and I knew that regardless of what happened, I was going to be okay.

As it turns out, the approach also worked remarkably well. Honesty and openness—go figure.

These very values have been the foundation of the relationship that I still share today with my husband.

Once we realized that we had something quite special, worth pursuing further, we took steps in line with our values of "integrity," "honesty," and "openness." My husband went directly to his boss, the president of the company, and his peers, sharing the information that we'd chosen to pursue a relationship. I'd agreed to obtain a position at another organization and was given a glowing letter of recommendation.

We managed everything with the utmost integrity, and colleagues, while sad to see me go, were happy for us both. We've now been married for over 17 years.

So, yes, it's unquestionably worth it to stand up for and live your values daily. If you're a runner, you might know what it's like to get a "runner's high." Well, standing up for your values is similar. It's like a huge rush of endorphins coursing through your body. Also, just like running, it's not easy, but dare I say, it can be addicting.

Taking Action

Okay, now it's your turn.

The time has come for you to identify your core values and take them out of hiding and bring them into the light. It's time for you to get crystal clear on what matters most to you, and what you deem as important at this point in your life. It's time for you to recognize how your values show up in your life and determine how you can live them daily.

It's essential to remember that your core values are just that—yours. They're not what others think you should value or care about, but only what you truly care about. Keep that in mind as well: your core values are not what you think you *should* value. Your core values are what you deem as most important to you, period.

When I did the following activity in workshops, people used to ask me, "Should I focus on work or my life outside of work?"

What do you think about that question?

If you said, "You don't have a set of core values for your professional life, and a separate set for your life outside of work," then you are right! If your core values are truly that, they stay the same regardless. They guide you in all aspects of your life, no matter what it is.

So here we go.

It's time for you to determine what you value most, to solve the puzzle that enables you to move closer to claiming your SWAGGER.

I should note, if you're thinking that you'll skip this part and come back to it later, think again! Remember that your SWAGGER doesn't exist without your core values, and your SWAGGER is waiting and won't be ignored.

So get to it.

Activity: Identifying Your Core Values
Time: 30 minutes

In this activity, you'll review a list of values and force-sort them into different categories, ultimately narrowing them down into your top five core values.

Step 1

Create four columns with the following headings on a piece of paper or in a digital document. Use whichever medium is most comfortable for you. Make sure there's space to record a list of values beneath each heading.

ALWAYS VALUED	FREQUENTLY VALUED	OCCASIONALLY VALUED	RARELY VALUED

Step 2

Review the following list of values. If you find that there's something you highly value and it's not listed, make sure to add it to the list before moving to step 3.

Acceptance	Courage	Gratitude	Perseverance
Achievement	Creativity	Harmony	Pleasure
Advancement	Curiosity	Helpfulness	Power
Adventure	Development	Honesty	Prosperity
Appreciation	Discipline	Humor	Quality
Authority	Empathy	Ingenuity	Recognition
Balance	Equality	Integrity	Reliability
Beauty	Excellence	Intimacy	Respect
Belonging	Fairness	Kindness	Security
Challenge	Faith	Knowledge	Service
Communication	Family	Learning	Stability
Community	Forgiveness	Logic	Status
Competence	Freedom	Loyalty	Teamwork
Competition	Friendship	Openness	Tradition
Consensus	Fun	Order	Well-being
Conservation	Generosity	Peace	Wisdom

Step 3

Record each value under one category that indicates how important that value is in your life right now.

Please note, you may record a maximum of 10 values in the *Always Valued* and *Frequently Valued* columns, respectively. Place the remaining values under *Occasionally Valued* or *Rarely Valued* columns. This will take some time, and you might need to move some values back and forth between columns.

This is called a "forced sort," and it's meant to be challenging. You might feel like all of the values are important, but every value can't fall into the *Always* or *Frequently Valued* columns.

You must make some tough choices and be brutally honest with yourself. Make sure to ask yourself whether this is something you truly value or something you think others believe you should value. Take your time and challenge your selections.

I also suggest completing your sort and putting it aside. Come back to it another time and see if you still feel the same way.

See the example below:

ALWAYS VALUED	FREQUENTLY VALUED	OCCASIONALLY VALUED	RARELY VALUED
Respect	Fun	Balance	Authority
Fairness	Challenge	Prosperity	Power
Honesty	Competence	Quality	Status
Courage	Service	Security	Integrity
Perseverance	Reliability	Stability	Well-being
Loyalty	Achievement	Teamwork	Conservation
Freedom	Adventure	Tradition	Beauty
Development	Generosity	Wisdom	Creativity
Learning	Appreciation	Recognition	Curiosity
Excellence	Pleasure	Logic	Discipline

		Openness	Knowledge
		Peace	Kindness
		Order	Consensus
		Humor	Intimacy
		Ingenuity	Belonging
		Helpfulness	Communication
		Harmony	Competition
		Gratitude	Community
		Forgiveness	Advancement
		Empathy	Acceptance
		Equality	Family
		Faith	Friendship

Step 4

Focus on your *Always Valued* column. Out of the ten values listed, highlight the five that are most vital to you at this time in your life. These are your top five core values.

Now rank these five values in order of importance. Begin with your top value and work your way down to five. Make sure to keep these top five values handy. You'll be using them as you continue along your SWAGGER journey.

Activity: Your Values in Action
Time: 20–30 minutes

Now that you've identified your top five core values, it's time to explore how they show up in your daily life.

Step 1

Determine and record a principle that corresponds to each value listed in your top five. As I said earlier, your core values influence your principles which guide your daily decisions and actions.

See the example below:

Value	**Principle**
Perseverance	*I will never give up. I will always finish what I started.*

Step 2

Answer and reflect on the following questions:

- How do my top five values and corresponding principles show up in my daily actions and decisions? Record an example.
- What happens to my behavior when my values are violated? Describe an example.

Daily Reinforcement: Raising Awareness
Time: 10 minutes

To get better at living your values, you must first become more aware of when and how they show up in your daily life. This reinforcement helps you identify examples throughout your day where your values shaped your behavior.

Step 1

Find a quiet place that's conducive to reflective work and a setting that enables you to write and record your thoughts.

Step 2

Start a values journal.

- Don't roll your eyes at me. How do I know you're rolling your eyes? Because I'd be the one rolling my eyes if someone asked me to do this. I'm an action-oriented person, so journaling isn't necessarily one of my favorite activities. Just know that everything I ask you to do has a purpose.

  o Think of it this way. What's the first thing a person is asked to do when they work with a dietitian? Record a daily food intake. Why? One, it promotes awareness, and two, it holds the person accountable. You can't just say, "I did a great job with what I ate yesterday." Your food intake diary might say otherwise.

  o The activity of journaling will increase your awareness, and help you get better at utilizing your core values. It'll help you see the many aspects of your life where your core values show up. Remember, core values are like muscles; they perform best when worked and strengthened regularly.

- This doesn't have to take long. Each day, record how your values impacted your decisions and actions. You decide when it makes the most sense for you. Throughout the day, you can simply jot down an example or experience where your values were evident. Or you can take a few minutes at the end of your day to reflect and identify some examples of how your values shaped your actions.

Daily Reinforcement: Shining a Light
Time: 10 minutes

To become more consistent in living your values, you have to understand when and why you act in conflict with them. This daily reinforcement helps you shine a light on what causes you to behave in ways that aren't aligned with your values so you can identify a better way forward.

Step 1

Think about times when you've acted in ways that don't reflect your values. Record in your journal what happened, and how you felt.

For example, perhaps you value kindness, and you find yourself behaving in line with this value quite often. However, there are some people or situations where you act out, you're mean to the other person, and you criticize instead of being kind. What do you say to yourself? How do you justify your actions even when they don't align with your values?

Step 2

Focus on one of the times you acted in a way that was contrary to your values.

What feelings or emotions were present? What needs were you working to fulfill? For example, perhaps you value loyalty, and you find yourself flirting with other people even though you're happily married. You're trying to satisfy the need to feel attractive and sexy. How could you satisfy those needs in other ways and still align with your values?

 ## SWAGGER Insight

- Your core values create a foundation for your SWAGGER and form an anchor that enables your SWAGGER to thrive.
- Without your core values, your SWAGGER can't exist.
- You already have core values; however, they might be hidden away for safekeeping.
- An organization's core values tell you who they are and how they behave.
- Your strengths, life experiences, and values influence your decisions, actions, and behaviors.
- Your core values are intimately connected to your needs and what you deem as important in your life.

- Your core values are the most powerful motivators for personal action and play a vital role as your internal compass, which guides your decisions and actions.
- You don't just make decisions based on "gut feelings." Rather, you use your core value to guide you in making informed decisions aligned with your values.
- Your core values are fundamental to who you are and how you engage with the world.
- Your core values are influenced by experiences, education, religion, and culture and can evolve over time based on whatever stage of life you're in.
- Your core values are personal, and therefore unique to you.
- When you make decisions while your core values are missing in action, frustration, anger, guilt, stress, and other negative responses await you.
- Your core values are like muscles; they function best when exercised regularly. The more you use them, the stronger they become and the more guidance they provide. Just like muscles, your core values can weaken and atrophy from lack of use.
- When you consistently use your core values to guide your daily actions and help you make decisions, you strengthen the neural pathways that make them easier to access.
- The more you intentionally use your core values, the more they become part of your everyday life.
- Beliefs are assumptions, things you hold to be true.
- Your beliefs help you navigate the world around you.
- Your beliefs, the assumptions you hold to be true, create the foundations upon which your values are formed.
- Principles tend to be less subjective and more unyielding, often employing qualitative words like "always" and "never."
- Principles help you distinguish between right and wrong, thus guiding your behavior.
- Your values inform your principles.

- Your **beliefs** are the assumptions that help you navigate the world around you and aid in shaping your **values**. Your **values** define what's important to you and inform your **principles**. Your **principles** are the rules that govern your *behavior*.

- **Beliefs** → *shape your* → **Values** → *inform your* → **Principles** → *govern your* → **Behavior**

- Bruised and wounded values can elicit painful emotional experiences.

- When you become aware that your values are what often cause you to get upset, hurt, or angry, you create options. You can choose how you'd like to respond when faced with similar situations in the future.

- You're at greater risk of getting your values hurt when you neglect to share them with others.

- Making assumptions about other people's values gets you nowhere and sends you directly into a never-ending spiral of unnecessary anger, frustration, and hurt.

- Unless your values are shared and communicated, people can't possibly know what they are.

- Just knowing what your core values are isn't enough. You have to live them. Daily.

- Living your values takes courage and a willingness to be bold. You have to be willing to stand up and live your values, regardless of whether or not they're popular or other people agree with them.

- It's scary to bring your values out into the open and lay them on the line, to share things that are so personal and open yourself up to getting hurt.

- When you put on that battle armor, or that superhero cape, and get past the initial fear, when you're daring enough to live your values, you're going to feel a hundred feet tall and bulletproof.

- When you're willing to live your values, you're telling yourself that you matter; that what you *value* matters. It's like a shot of adrenaline for your self-worth, and a booster shot for your SWAGGER.

- When you're about to do something that scares you, it's a pretty good indication that you're getting ready to put yourself in a vulnerable position and live your values.
- You know you're getting ready to live your values when you experience the fear that makes you question whether or not it's the right thing to do, and you have no idea how what you're going to do or say will be received.
- It's unquestionably worth it to stand up for and live your values daily. While it's not easy, the rush you get from doing it can be addicting.

CHAPTER 7

Empowering Yourself to Overcome Self-Limiting Beliefs

Picture this:

You're poised in the starting blocks, ready to race. The gun fires and everyone else around you explodes out of the blocks like rockets blasting off. For some reason, you find it impossible to move. You're trapped, restrained by chains holding you to the blocks. You can't seem to get your feet out of the blocks no matter how hard you try. The rest of the field continues to pull away from you until they're no longer even in view.

So you decide to shift your focus off everyone else and onto the finish line—your goals and dreams—just ahead of you. They're so close. If you can just focus and try harder, you know you can make it. However, with each failed attempt, nothing changes. You're still on the starting blocks, unable to move. You try everything in your power, but you can't figure out how to break free of the chains holding you back.

Have you ever felt like this?

Have you ever experienced the sensation that everyone around you is steadily moving forward in life, toward goals, and accomplishing their dreams? All the while, you're stuck at the starting line, hoping for a miracle?

Yeah, I'm sure you have. Don't worry. Because I have too.

The first thing I can tell you is, hope is not a winning strategy, my friend. Hoping, or wishing, will do nothing to release you from those chains; it'll do nothing to get you off those starting blocks.

But what would you say if I told you that you already had the key to unlock the chains that are holding you back?

Would you believe me?

Okay, maybe not, but you're intrigued, aren't you?

Good. Because what I'm telling you is true. You hold the key to those chains; you just haven't learned how to use it. You have everything you need to not only break free from the chains but unleash your potential and achieve everything you once deemed impossible.

How do I know this?

Well for one, I'm living proof. Two, I know exactly what those chains are, and the actual winning strategy to keep them from holding you back ever again.

Have you figured it out yet?

I'm sure you have, and you'd be absolutely correct. Those chains holding you back are your self-limiting beliefs. Or, rather, what I like to call your "SWAGGER-limiting beliefs." These limiting beliefs are the very things that keep you from tapping into what makes you unique and extraordinary, being your best self, performing at your best, and living your best life.

But guess what? The days of these beliefs getting in your way stop right here and right now. In this chapter, you'll uncover the SWAGGER-limiting beliefs you fall victim to most and where they came from, and I'll teach you a strategy to overcome them whenever they show up uninvited.

How's that sound? Shall we begin?

The Uninvited Guest

SWAGGER-limiting beliefs don't care how wealthy, intelligent, or successful you are. They're not picky; they show up regardless.

Take a look at the most accomplished person you know, and you can bet that they too have SWAGGER-limiting beliefs. Heck, that's betting on a sure thing, like you put all of your money on black at the roulette wheel, only to realize that *all* the numbers are black.

But SWAGGER-limiting beliefs are uninvited guests. No one asked them to come to the party, but they showed up anyway. It doesn't matter if you have security checking names and invitations at the velvet ropes, SWAGGER-limiting beliefs arrive and say, "Oh, I'm just so sure I'm on the list. I'm extremely close friends with the host. Just let them know that I'm here. I'm certain they'll give you the green light to let me in."

The problem is, most of the time, SWAGGER-limiting beliefs are *right*. We do let them in, and they wreak havoc, ruining the party, and our lives.

One of the most interesting phenomena I've encountered with leaders I've worked with was the uninvited guest that they almost always let in—a common thread with leaders from all walks of life. Once they became leaders, a certain SWAGGER-limiting belief showed up that apparently was required to attend the party: the belief that they had to have all the answers. The crazy notion that if they didn't know everything, then they were somehow an ill-equipped leader crept inside them and kept them from excelling in the role.

What's more, SWAGGER-limiting beliefs are also the uninvited guests that always seem to arrive at the most inopportune time. But before you can place those uninvited guests on the "Do Not Admit" list, you must first be able to clearly identify them.

So now it's time to call them out.

Below is a list of common SWAGGER-limiting beliefs. Read through each statement and make note of the ones that show up most frequently for you. If you're anything like me, you'll note quite a few. If you have some SWAGGER-limiting beliefs that aren't listed, be sure to record those as well. Just remember that there are no wrong answers here. You've got to be able to name your uninvited guests so that you know who to watch out for going forward.

SWAGGER-Limiting Beliefs

- I can't because . . .
- I'm not good/smart/experienced, etc. enough.
- I'm too old/young, etc.
- Good things only happen to other people.
- I don't have time.
- I'm not worthy enough.
- Bad things always happen to me.
- People will judge me or think poorly of me.
- I don't deserve to be happy/loved/successful, etc.
- I'll never be successful/happy, etc.
- Sure, they can do it, but I'll never be able to.
- I'll never be good/smart/thin, etc. enough.
- If I can't do it perfectly/exceptionally well, then why bother.
- I'm a failure.
- I'll never be as good as them.
- I'm an idiot.
- I'm afraid I'll fail.
- This is my life, I just have to accept it.
- I'm just waiting for the other shoe to drop, it always does.
- I'm not good at that.

How was that?

It's pretty strange to come face-to-face with these uninvited guests, isn't it? The phrases that you noted are likely familiar, but they probably aren't normally out there in the open, in black in white for all the world to see. It might make them seem more real. Or it might even make them seem more sinister, doesn't it? You could even be asking, "Wow, do I really say those things to myself?"

It's extraordinary to think that we allow these uninvited guests to come to our party and treat us in this manner. I mean, there is no way we'd ever allow any *person* to say things that hurtful to our family or friends. There's no possible scenario in which we'd tolerate that kind of talk from anyone else. So why do we allow them to keep showing up, treating us like this, and wreaking havoc on our lives?

It's a great and complex question, so let's dig into that as we take a closer look at where these SWAGGER-limiting beliefs come from.

Where Are You From?

"Where are you from?"

It's such a simple phrase that we use all the time. It's one of the most common things we might ask someone when we first meet them.

However, when was the last time you asked your uninvited guests, the SWAGGER-limiting beliefs, where they were from?

Part of being able to overcome these beliefs is understanding where they come from, and how and why they started showing up in the first place.

Let's start by breaking down the term.

"Self-limiting" or, for our purposes, "SWAGGER-limiting," is exactly what it sounds like. This means that what this is describing is *limiting* your ability to reach and achieve your goals—be your best self, live your best life, etcetera.

But what about the word "beliefs"? We first addressed beliefs back in Chapter 6, remember? Beliefs are assumptions; they are things you hold to be true. Now, beliefs may or may not have scientific proof. The fact is, you simply believe them. So, in regard to what we're discussing, these are beliefs that you hold about yourself, regardless of who may have initiated them.

This all makes perfect sense so far, right?

Okay, so then, how do these beliefs start in the first place? Well, that's the tricky part. Are you sitting down? Good, because this might come as a complete shock . . .

Your SWAGGER-limiting beliefs originated *to protect you. That's right, these uninvited guests originated to protect you* from pain and suffering.

I know, it seems crazy, doesn't it?

How can something so detrimental to you now have begun with the intention to help you? It just doesn't make sense. So let's see if we can take the crazy down a notch by expanding your understanding.

Back in Chapter 5 we discussed how your life experiences, and the stories you tell yourself about those experiences, shape who you are and how you show up today. Well, the intense emotions that you connect with those experiences create powerful memories and, ultimately, directly influence your SWAGGER-limiting beliefs.

Let me show you what I mean.

Geordie was largely raised by his mother. His parents divorced when he was only four years old, and his father, who was rarely present in his life, always made promises to visit but failed to keep them.

Geordie would wait with anticipation by the window on the days that his father was to come. He would spend the whole day waiting, hoping, and wishing for his father to show. Each time, his father failed to appear, and Geordie's heart would break all over again, releasing powerful feelings of loss, rejection, and sadness.

The story Geordie told himself about this experience was that he was to blame for his father not showing up. That had to be the reason. I mean, why would his father continue to break his promises if Geordie hadn't done something? It couldn't possibly be that his father was selfish, incapable of getting his life together, or only focused on his own needs, right? No, there had to be another reason. Because his father, who Geordie idolized, couldn't be at fault; it must be his own fault.

Over time, Geordie developed a coping mechanism to keep himself from getting hurt. He would tell himself a single narrative on repeat: "Dad isn't going to show up, so why get your hopes up? You know why he isn't coming, don't you? You're not worthy of his love or his time. Why would he show up for someone so undeserving? Maybe if you were a better son or performed better in school or sports, he might want to spend time with you. The sooner you realize that you're not worthy, the better off you'll be. Then you won't keep wishing and hoping for something that will never happen."

Now, Geordie's SWAGGER-limiting belief started at a very young age to protect him from the continual hurt of his father's broken promises. Therefore, his brain categorized this repeated experience as trauma and helped create this narrative because it wanted to protect him against future pain and suffering.

Let's look at another example.

Jordan is the youngest of two girls. Both she and her older sister were bright and excelled in school. Jordan was a bit of a tomboy in her younger years. She focused much of her time on competing and excelling in various sports. Her older sister Audrey, on the other hand, pursued activities like dance and was highly focused on staying in shape and keeping her physique in top condition. She spent countless hours exercising and always worked to look her best, no matter where she was going. Jordan noticed that wherever they went, her sister was regularly complimented for her beauty.

Unlike her sister, Jordan struggled with her weight. She tried various diets and exercise routines, but nothing ever really worked for her. She was no less beautiful than her sister, they were just built differently. But it's human nature to make comparisons, and this case is no different.

People frequently asked Jordan why she didn't look like her sister, which did nothing to help her self-image. This filled Jordan with feelings of hurt, rejection, and mortification. Because of the constant comparisons to her sister, Jordan developed the belief that she wasn't beautiful and would never be seen that way by others. Jordan created a SWAGGER-limiting belief to protect herself from those cruel feelings. "You're never going to be thought of as beautiful," she told herself. "You should just focus on being the smart girl, the funny girl, or the athletic girl. You'll never be as pretty as other people, so why bother trying? Just accept the fact that you're not attractive and move on."

Jordan's brain had identified this experience as harmful to her and created the SWAGGER-limiting belief to shield her from an overly critical and superficial world that she knew to be only focused on beauty.

Is any of this striking a chord with you?

Sometimes, SWAGGER-limiting beliefs come from a person of authority or someone you look up to. When a parent, teacher, coach, or employer says something to you enough times, you begin to believe it. Perhaps your mother called you an idiot and berated you for making mistakes. Maybe your coach told you that you'd never be good enough to play, or your teacher called you worthless and said you'd never amount to anything.

For me, it was a riding instructor I worked with that I highly respected, and this happened recently—not in my youth. That's the thing about SWAGGER-limiting beliefs, by the way, they don't just formulate when we're young. They're always lurking beneath the surface, ready to jump in and "save" the day.

Anyway, this instructor told me, in no uncertain terms, that I'd never be able to ride my young horses. She didn't think I'd ever have the right mindset and skill level to be the rider these horses needed me to be. I remember driving home from the barn in tears, thinking that the dream I'd envisioned since childhood was lost forever.

The seed she planted fed into my own insecurities and the SWAGGER-limiting beliefs I'd created as a child. True to form, my uninvited guests showed up in force to provide armor and protection from being hurt. I created a new SWAGGER-limiting belief around this experience and started saying it to myself, because I certainly didn't want to continue letting her make me feel unworthy and incapable of doing what I'd dreamed of for so long.

"I'm not good enough," I told myself. "They need a stronger and more confident rider than me. Maybe if I'd started riding at a younger age, things might be different. Perhaps I should sell my horses and stop this insanity. I need to face the facts. I'll never be capable of being what they need me to be."

To protect ourselves from feeling ridiculed and belittled by these authority figures in the future, we take on that role ourselves, short-circuiting the process. Then, our SWAGGER-limiting beliefs come to the rescue. But that's the danger with SWAGGER-limiting beliefs: they're born out of fear. Fear of getting hurt, fear of failing, fear of being judged, and on and on and on.

While these uninvited guests begin as our protectors, friends, the things we trust to help us survive the dangers of childhood and our young adult lives, the more we trust in them and the more power we give to them, the more they control the trajectory of our lives.

But don't let this get you down because things aren't always what they appear to be.

Peeking Behind the Curtain

Remember the movie *The Wizard of Oz*?

Do you remember what happened when Dorothy, the Tin Man, the Scarecrow, and the Cowardly Lion finally arrived at the Emerald City and met the Wizard?

Like many who probably came before them, they were frightened and awestruck by the mighty Wizard. However, when they were able to peek behind the curtain, they realized that the all-powerful Wizard turned out to be nothing more than an ordinary man cleverly using parlor tricks to appear magical and larger than life.

So that's what we have to ask about your SWAGGER-limiting beliefs—are they friend or foe? They masquerade as a trusted protector and ally, but are they truly? Perhaps you should consider them more as an enemy than your friend.

You've likely heard the phrase "keep your friends close and your enemies closer." Well, it's time to peek behind that curtain and get to know your uninvited guests a little more. It's time to unmask your SWAGGER-limiting beliefs and put their claims to the test.

In her book *Multipliers*, CEO and best-selling author, Liz Wiseman, identified two kinds of leaders. She called leaders either "Multipliers" or "Diminishers."

Multiplier leaders challenge, develop, and grow those they lead. In contrast, Diminisher leaders create environments where the potential of those they lead is untapped and unrealized. Liz found that while both types of leaders do many things the same, there are fundamental differences in the way they see the world and how they behave.

As a Certified Multipliers Facilitator, I've spent a lot of time studying and educating leaders around these concepts. Recently, I made a fascinating discovery of my own. SWAGGER-limiting beliefs behave very much the same as Diminisher leaders do. In fact, I'd say that the parallels are uncanny.

Your SWAGGER-limiting beliefs are certain that you can't possibly figure things out on your own or survive without them. They are know-it-alls, telling you what's good for you and what you should avoid. With them, the decision has already been made, there's no debate. You're not good enough, smart enough, or capable of doing whatever it is you're contemplating. They're the happiest when you allow them to be involved in and manage every detail of your life. The stress they create is what keeps you from challenging yourself and doing your best thinking, causing you to underutilize your talent and potential.

This is very aligned with what Liz Wiseman found to be true of Diminisher leaders in her research. What she also found to be true was that people who worked for Diminisher leaders only gave about half of what they were capable of.

So under closer examination, it seems that your SWAGGER-limiting beliefs are not your protectors, or your friends, as they claim to be. Instead, they're behaving much more like a Diminisher leader. As such, they diminish your ability to utilize your full potential and live your life at your highest capacity.

In addition to behaving like a Diminisher leader, your SWAGGER-limiting beliefs work from what Carol Dweck would call a "fixed mindset." Dweck is an author, psychologist, and professor at Stanford

University. In her book *Mindset: The New Psychology of Success*, she categorizes individuals as having one of two mindsets—either "growth" or "fixed"—based on their beliefs around learning and intelligence.

People with a growth mindset believe that you're constantly learning, and that intelligence can be improved with time and effort. Contrary to this, people working from a fixed mindset tend to believe that intelligence is static, that you can't change or improve from where you are today, and that learning new skills is pointless.

I've become familiar with Dweck's work around growth and fixed mindsets. Many of the leadership workshops I've designed have included activities aimed at shifting from fixed to growth mindset. That's why, as we peek behind the curtain and look more closely, it became clear to me that SWAGGER-limiting beliefs are firmly grounded in a fixed mindset.

To the uninvited guests, things are immovable, set in stone. You're either capable, or you're not. Period, full stop. This mindset creates a tendency for you to be cautious and conservative, to hold back, to be happy with the status quo. In this mindset, you might find yourself getting stuck in the moment and blaming others for your inability to achieve greatness . . .

> "Things might be different if only I'd been given better opportunities" or "Sure, they succeeded, but that's because they didn't have my upbringing" or "It's not my fault that I'm not good at that" or "This is all that a person like me can hope to achieve."

Do any of these sound familiar? Yeah, I know. Your SWAGGER-limiting beliefs are pretty sneaky and really good at getting you to believe what they're saying. One thing is for sure, a good friend and someone with your best interests in mind would never behave in this way. They wouldn't allow you to remain stuck in your fixed mindset or limit your ability to fully step into your potential.

Behaving like a Diminisher leader and working from a fixed mindset, SWAGGER-limiting beliefs do more to undermine you than help you. It's even what made me think they were akin to what author and lecturer, Shirzad Chamine, calls "saboteurs" in his book *Positive Intelligence*.

"Saboteurs?" you ask. That's right.

You know, like in the movies when the engineer sabotages the propulsion system of the submarine, compromising the mission? The only difference is your SWAGGER-limiting beliefs are saboteurs coming from inside your head.

In his research, Chamine identified nine saboteurs constantly working to undermine you at every turn. They're what cause you to relapse to old patterns of behavior and fall short of achieving your true potential for happiness and success. It's not because you're incapable of change; it's because your saboteurs are preventing you from sticking with the desired change long enough to form a new habit.

Much like your SWAGGER-limiting beliefs, these saboteurs influence how you view yourself and others, define your circumstances, engage with the world around you, and perform in life. Because they believe that you can't succeed without them, they've worked tirelessly over the years to be seen as your trusted partner, at the helm of your advisory board.

See the ongoing similarities here? It seems that the more we look behind the curtain, the more we uncover information to directly refute any unsubstantiated claims of your SWAGGER-limiting beliefs.

Best-selling author and noted psychology professor Martin Seligman would probably agree. In fact, he might go so far as to suggest that if SWAGGER-limiting beliefs are left to take root, they could lead to depression, even helplessness.

Based on Professor Seligman's research, SWAGGER-limiting beliefs could definitely be categorized as using a "pessimistic explanatory style." In his book, *Learned Optimism*, he defines "explanatory style" as the way in which you consistently explain to yourself why events happen. With a pessimistic explanatory style, explanations of events often center around you, placing the blame or fault squarely on your shoulders . . .

"It's all my fault" or "That happened because I'm such an idiot" or "Of course that happened, I'm a total failure."

Sound familiar?

In addition, a pessimistic explanatory style describes situations and events with a sense of permanence, frequently using broad generalities and universal statements . . .

"Bad things always happen to me" or "It's never going to get better" or "This is going to ruin everything" or "All that I've worked so hard for is gone forever."

Your SWAGGER-limiting beliefs are adept at using this pessimistic explanatory style. It doesn't matter if you're an optimist or pessimist, your logical brain can be hijacked by these statements at any time. Consistently using a pessimistic explanatory style is a precursor to depression. Additionally, the steady stream of destructive thoughts that these uninvited guests bring with them plant the seeds that foster helplessness.

Wow, such an expressive word, isn't it? "Helplessness." It's almost as if you've been punched in the gut just reading it. You can automatically visualize someone with their head hung so low and shoulders sloped in resignation.

Helplessness is often defined as the feeling or state of being unable to do anything to help yourself or anyone else. In Seligman's research, he found that helplessness can be learned. "Learned helplessness" is when you quit and give up because you believe that there's nothing you can do to change your situation or circumstances. You believe wholeheartedly that no matter what you do, it won't make one bit of difference.

Would a friend or someone who truly cares about you lead you down a path toward helplessness? No, I don't think so. Yet, that's exactly what your SWAGGER-limiting beliefs do when you invite them in and allow them to provide you counsel.

So how are you seeing your SWAGGER-limiting beliefs? Do you still accept the idea that they're your protector or your friend? Do you think they're looking out for your best interests?

Hopefully, this chance to peek behind the curtain has uncovered evidence that makes you question their claims. Perhaps you should start thinking of them as Public Enemy Number One, or more aptly put, SWAGGER Enemy Number One.

Better yet, why not start asking yourself some different questions?

What do you think might be possible if you were able to reduce the diminishing effect of your SWAGGER-limiting beliefs? What could you create if you adopted a growth mindset and stopped allowing your SWAGGER-limiting beliefs to sabotage your efforts? What would your life look like if you were able to change the destructive things you say to yourself when you experience setbacks?

These are all great questions to ponder, but we've got more to do before you start answering them.

Assessing the Damage

Ever had a party at your home where you enjoyed yourself a bit too much? You decided to worry about cleanup the day after, and when you woke up the following morning, you walked into the kitchen and had to evaluate exactly how long it was going to take to restore order.

Well, that's where we are right now.

You see, we've allowed these uninvited guests to our party one too many times, and they've caused mayhem. Now we have to take time to assess the damage these SWAGGER-limiting beliefs have left behind.

Let's explore what happens when and if we continue to give these uninvited guests free passes to do what they want.

Since looking at a whole picture can be overwhelming, you might not even know where to start. So to tackle a job like this, it's perhaps more useful to break it into smaller chunks and focus on one part at a time.

In this case, we'll look at the damage SWAGGER-limiting beliefs have caused as it relates to self, engaging with others, and performing in life.

Before you look at others, it's best to take a look at yourself first, so let's start there.

It's pretty easy to see that SWAGGER-limiting beliefs can cause significant damage to your self-worth—it's death by a thousand cuts. Each time these uninvited guests show up, they take a piece of your self-worth with them until, eventually, there's nothing left. As we will recall from Chapter 3, your self-worth is strongly connected to your self-esteem and self-confidence.

The words "I am," "I'm not," and "I don't deserve" are statements about your identity and who you believe you are. It doesn't matter if you say them in earnest or jest, your subconscious pays attention to every word. Each time you use these phrases, it's a lethal blow to your self-worth making it even more vulnerable to continued damage. Sustained damage to your self-worth can lead to severe depression, helplessness, even suicide.

Let's revisit Geordie's story.

Geordie believed he wasn't good enough and didn't deserve his dad's time and affection. If a narrative like that goes unchecked, it can expand into other areas of life. Geordie might start to believe that he doesn't deserve success, happiness, or at the most extreme, being alive. You can see the possibility for the damage to his self-worth to spiral out of control.

Furthermore, when your self-worth is damaged, it also directly affects how you engage with others. Your SWAGGER-limiting beliefs are like self-fulfilling prophecies. For example, if you don't believe that you're worthy of love, then you won't attract and find relationships where you can be loved.

This is often what happens in abusive relationships. The person being abused doesn't believe they're worthy or deserving of love and affection. They can believe so strongly that they've done something to earn the abuse and treatment they receive that they might even welcome the abuse, thinking it's meant to help them.

What's more, these self-fulfilling prophecies can jeopardize your performance and cause chaos in the rest of your life as well. If you don't think you're good with money, then you might find yourself in a perpetual state of financial calamity. If you blame yourself or think you're an idiot for making mistakes, then you'll avoid situations where there's a potential to make mistakes.

A great example of this is from the 1986 movie *Top Gun*. F-14 fighter pilot Maverick loses his Radar Intercept Officer, Goose, during a training exercise. Even though he was not found to be at fault for the accident, Maverick blames himself and falls into despair. When Maverick finally returns to flying, he's unable to take the necessary risks required to engage in combat. He makes excuses and avoids all situations that might lead to additional mistakes. This makes him utterly ineffective and useless as a fighter pilot. In this situation, his SWAGGER-limiting beliefs were completely sabotaging his abilities and limiting his potential.

Like Maverick, you can become paralyzed by the fear your SWAGGER-limiting beliefs create. You can find yourself caught in the unending negative spiral of believing that the worst is about to happen. Even when things go well, you're waiting for the next shoe to drop, because you feel deep down that it's going to.

As an example, Simon falls into this category. He just received news from his doctor that he has something on his prostate that they'd like to take a closer look at. While he has no idea what it is, he automatically assumes the worst and is convinced that his doctor is going to tell him he has cancer. His mind goes into a death spiral, wondering how bad it's going to be and how much time he'll have left to live. "What will happen to my family? How will they cope? What should I do with the time I have left?" He's certain he's dying. These destructive thoughts hijack his logical brain and keep him up at night.

As it turns out, Simon did not have cancer at all. But, if his SWAGGER-limiting beliefs were allowed to continue longer, the stress and anxiety they produced could've very likely manifested into physical illness. It's important to remember that the mind has a powerful impact on the body. The way you think about your health can directly affect it. If you think the worst will happen, you better believe you can make the worst happen.

Another self-fulfilling prophecy revolves around the belief that you're not good enough. If you don't believe you're good enough or smart enough, then you certainly aren't going to let yourself apply to that hard-to-get-into college, take challenging risks, or chase that promotion. This belief handcuffs you to the status quo, limits your potential, and safely keeps you inside your comfort zone, far away from challenges and opportunities that move you closer to your dreams.

Your SWAGGER-limiting beliefs continually encourage you to underutilize your potential, holding you back, putting you in your own way, and keeping you from fully stepping into who you're capable of being. As a consequence, fulfilling relationships, a rewarding career, and a gratifying life will elude you and go unrealized.

I'm a perfect example of this.

For the longest time, I didn't think I was a good writer. That's one of the reasons it took me so long to realize my dream of writing this book.

When I was given a writing assignment in school, I would spend countless hours unable to write a single word, staring down at a blank piece of paper (yes, we did indeed write on paper back then). Oh, and do you remember my severe test anxiety from Chapter 5? Well, that triggered the belief that I needed to be perfect, and that nothing less than perfection would do.

The tentacles of my perfectionist tendencies touched numerous areas of my life, including writing. For some reason, I believed that the words I wrote needed to be perfect from the start. The idea of writing something and then revising it just didn't seem to work for me. Even to this day, I still struggle with this. Starting a chapter is one of the hardest things for me to do. I stare, hopefully, almost prayerfully, for what can seem like an eternity, at the blank word processing document on the computer screen.

To say that it's a constant battle is an understatement, however, it's one that I'm learning to win. I force myself to write, to just capture whatever thoughts come into my head. I often find the need to encourage and coach myself out loud. A fly on the wall would have a giggle of a time watching me write, in fact. Of course, I logically know that I can rework and revise the words as I go, but this deep-rooted belief is still there and hard to shake. Thank goodness there are these miraculous people called editors who can help me transform something good into something even better.

Now to the other reasons why it's taken me so long to write this book: do you know that I began formulating my first ideas for this book way back in 2008? It just floors me when I think about this. Mind you, many things needed to happen for me to be ready and able to write this today, not least of which was going through my own SWAGGER journey. But the two main things that kept me from putting words down were simply the fear of failure and my impostor syndrome.

Yes, you read that correctly: fear of failure and impostor syndrome. Now, you might wonder to yourself, "How can someone who's writing a book about claiming your SWAGGER be plagued with fears of failure and impostor syndrome?"

Well, it's easy.

As someone with perfectionist tendencies, my bar for success can sometimes be unrealistically high and, therefore, even more challenging to reach. That's when fear kicks in.

"What if I fail? What if I don't succeed? What if my book doesn't sell? What if my book doesn't resonate with people and provide the education and help it's meant to?"

Fear is a powerful emotion, as I'm sure you're aware. It's also what fuels impostor syndrome. My impostor syndrome stems from my fear of being seen as a fraud, or someone unworthy of writing a book to help other people. My SWAGGER-limiting beliefs go into overdrive, and they're vicious. "Who are you to be writing a book?" they say. "What gives you the right? Who died and named you the expert? Why would people want to read anything you write?"

As I'm sure you're aware, it's not a pleasant experience being on the receiving end of those uninvited guests. They've certainly done a number on my self-worth, self-esteem, and self-confidence over the years, which I've spent a significant amount of time repairing. They've also kept me from unlocking my potential and taking the leap to live my dream of writing this book. I've chased and achieved many dreams in my life, but fourteen years is a long time to be kept in the starting blocks, unable to race toward this dream.

So what are you waiting for?

Don't take as long as I have to kick out your uninvited guests and live the life you've imagined.

Read on to learn how to disempower your SWAGGER-limiting beliefs and apply a winning strategy for combating them when they show up.

Taking Charge

Are you ready for some good news?

Okay, here it is: the only reason your SWAGGER-limiting beliefs have power and control is because you keep inviting them in.

Ready for some *even better* news?

You, and only you, can put those uninvited guests on the "Do Not Admit" list. You can deprive your SWAGGER-limiting beliefs of all their power and authority over you.

Sure, those nasty uninvited guests are going to keep showing up, as mine do, but you can learn how to be better prepared to send them packing the moment they arrive at your door.

Here's something else to remember: what you believe is what you create, and what others see. We just highlighted the self-fulfilling prophecies that your SWAGGER-limiting beliefs can generate, but remember that these beliefs are just that. Beliefs. They aren't statements of fact. They aren't the truth. You've simply chosen to believe them. Your SWAGGER-limiting beliefs are nothing more than habits about the way you currently think of yourself and your circumstances. These habits don't have to last forever. They're not a fait accompli. Did you know that you can choose the way you think?

Wait, what?

I know, it's a revelation. The idea that people can choose the way they think is one of the most significant findings in psychological research over the last two decades.

Yes, you can determine how you think. You can determine how you think about yourself, others, and your circumstances.

Guess what that means?

That means, you have a choice to make. You can decide to stay with your current status quo and continue to allow your SWAGGER-limiting beliefs to dictate your thoughts and remain unhappy, unfulfilled, or unsatisfied. Or you can take charge and make a shift. Do some spring cleaning and let go of the things that no longer serve you.

Keep this in mind:

You'll never be good enough, and things won't change unless you change the way you think, and what you say to yourself.

Now, I'm not saying that shifting the way you think is going to be easy here, but aren't you worth it? And don't you let your SWAGGER-limiting beliefs answer that question for you, by the way. I'll do it. Yes, you are worth it, and yes, you can do it.

But let me first say this. Sometimes there are weeds in your garden that keep coming back no matter what you do. You realize that you can't tackle these on your own and have to bring in an expert. Just like those weeds, some of your SWAGGER-limiting beliefs might involve incredibly hurtful memories, and these won't be so easy to uproot. Don't be afraid to seek professional assistance to support your efforts to work through these and create the desired shift in your thinking.

Things in life rarely go exactly as you plan, and setbacks are a given. These things are bound to happen along your journey. Creating a shift in your thinking isn't so much about saying nice things to yourself, but rather how you view the setbacks, the making mistakes, and the personal defeats as you progress forward. Once you shift the way you think, you can change the destructive things you say to yourself when faced with setbacks that inevitably happen.

But like a new pair of eyeglasses or contact lens, this calls for a change in perspective. So instead of looking through the pessimistic lens of a fixed mindset, try putting on a new pair of glasses and see what things look like through the optimistic lens of a growth mindset.

When you do, you might find that the experiences that previously appeared to be your fault, or had a sense of permanence, or seemed to impact all aspects of your life, were nothing more than essential opportunities for learning, growth, and development.

Let's look at some examples to illustrate this idea below:

Old Lens	New Lens
It's all my fault.	Yes, I made a mistake. What can I do going forward to ensure that doesn't happen again?
It's never going to get better.	Things will only change if I do something to change them, something different from what I'm doing today.
This is going to ruin everything.	No, it's not ideal, but we can work with this. Let's create a plan of attack given this new information.
I can't do that.	I don't yet have the skills to be able to do that. What do I need to learn to make it possible for me to do that?

See the shift here? Things look much brighter and more hopeful looking through the growth mindset lens, don't they? You're no longer viewing setbacks with a sense of permanence and pervasiveness. So instead of being stuck with nowhere to go, the new optimistic lens provides a more productive path forward, wherein you take ownership and control of what comes next.

I know. What a concept.

A word to the wise, though, taking ownership and control does mean that you can no longer blame others for the mistakes you make or your lot in life. Once you make the shift, you hold the reins. This can be a scary place to find yourself if you've not inhabited it much before. But don't panic. Just breathe and remember that pivoting to this new way of thinking will take our **P to the Power of 3 – Patience – Practice – Perseverance**. Your natural tendency will be to return back to your comfort zone, where you're used to residing. But that hasn't served you very well thus far. So, like moving out of a house you've outgrown, it's time to relocate to a new dwelling where you can stop just surviving and start thriving. Be patient with yourself, and continue to put in the practice and time, and whatever you do, don't give up.

Recently, I started physical therapy to rehabilitate my ankle, post-injury. One of the main points they emphasized, over and over again, was this: my participation and adherence to the treatment plan were vital to my successful recovery. If I don't do the exercises and I don't follow the protocol, my recovery will not happen.

The same is true for you. You have to practice, practice, practice, and practice some more, to create a full recovery from your destructive SWAGGER-limiting beliefs that have held you back for far too long.

What exactly will you be practicing you might be asking?

Let's explore your new winning strategy for overcoming your SWAGGER-limiting beliefs.

A Winning Strategy

So each exercise in my physical therapy treatment plan contains a specific number of *repetitions*—"reps" for short.

Since building strength and flexibility requires repetition, *reps*, and time, that's precisely what we're going to employ to help you overcome your SWAGGER-limiting beliefs.

You're going to learn to do **REP**s. In this case, **REP** stands for **Recog-nize**, **Evaluate**, and **Pivot**.

I know, here I go with my acronyms again—I just find them so helpful for remembering things. Hopefully, they'll be useful for you as well.

Right, so let's dig into this, shall we?

Recognize

The first step in the REP strategy is to **recognize**.

You have to learn to be vigilant and recognize when your SWAGGER-limiting beliefs show up. This step is all about asking yourself, "What?"

- <u>What</u> feelings or reactions do they generate?
- <u>What</u> triggers their arrival?
- <u>What</u> thoughts and statements run through your head?

When I say that you have to learn to be vigilant, I'm talking about strengthening your powers of observation. You can't move to the next step of the REP approach without first recognizing that your SWAGGER-limiting beliefs are present. The best way to do this is to pay attention to your body language, notice how you're feeling, and listen to what the voice inside your head is saying.

What do I mean by body language?

If you've ever watched a professional athletic event, particularly something like a tennis match, you've likely seen the body language that accompanies a SWAGGER-limiting belief hijacking. It's what takes place when a player misses a shot that costs them a critical point in the match, and then they can't ever recover.

First, you notice frustration illustrated by closing the eyes, tilting the head back, and maybe screaming. This is often followed by yelling at the player's box, supported by hand gestures, as if trying to plead a case. Next, you see a shaking of the head and anger starting to rise as even more mistakes are made. There is a banging of the racquet on the court. Last, you will see the shoulders slump, the energy wane, and resignation finally set in.

SWAGGER-limiting beliefs win that battle, and the player gives up, ultimately losing the set and the match.

This is what I mean by body language: paying attention to what you're feeling and how your body is responding to those feelings.

For example, are you angry, frustrated, hurt, ashamed, afraid? Do you tense up? Does your rate of breathing increase? Do your shoulders slump as if defeated? Does your heart rate speed up or slow down? Do you get hot or begin to perspire?

When you notice these physical changes in your body, you can ask yourself, "What triggered that? What just took place that caused that to happen?"

In our example with the tennis player, it's the missed shot or the mishit. That "mistake" was the trigger for the meltdown.

Once you've pinpointed a trigger, you can listen carefully to what the voice inside your head says. For our tennis player, it might sound like, "You idiot! I can't believe you just did that! There goes your chance. You just blew it. The match is over, so you might as well give up now."

Thus, the self-fulfilling prophecy strikes again.

Evaluate

The second step in REP is **evaluate**.

This is where you get to channel your inner high-powered attorney from your favorite courtroom drama.

As the high-powered attorney, you evaluate the claims your SWAGGER-limiting beliefs made by doing the following:

- <u>Search</u> for evidence to substantiate or refute the claims.
- <u>Play out</u> the worst-case scenario.
- <u>Determine</u> the usefulness of the claims.

As any high-powered attorney knows, the facts don't lie. The best way to refute a negative belief is to demonstrate that it's factually incorrect. You can ask yourself questions like, "What evidence do you have to support your claim?" or "What past examples can you share to support your think-ing?" or "What previous experiences cause you to believe this to be true?"

The unknown is frightening and can cause irrational fear. When you play out the worst-case scenario, you often come to find that it's not as bad as your fear imagined it to be. It might not be ideal, but it's certainly not the end of the world.

Last in the evaluation step is determining the usefulness of those claims (or beliefs).

Are the beliefs currently serving your best interests? Are they support-ing or helping you achieve what you're working to accomplish?

If the tennis player from our example had utilized REP and evaluated the claims their SWAGGER-limiting beliefs had made, it might sound something like this: "Yes, I made a mistake, but what evidence do I have that I'm an idiot and the match is over? We're only in the third set. Worst-case scenario, they take this set. That doesn't mean the match is over. These thoughts aren't helpful right now and are a waste of energy."

Pivot

The final step in REP is **pivot**.

Pivoting is all about shifting your thoughts and what you say to your-self to enable you to move forward more productively. We first introduced this concept in the previous section, "Taking Charge." The pivot means replacing your destructive thoughts with constructive ones.

Since your SWAGGER-limiting beliefs are quite sensitive and have a bit of an ego, it's helpful to incorporate this approach when working through this step.

Say, "Thank you."

Replace the destructive thought with a constructive one.

Now, saying "thank you" might seem like an odd way to begin this step of REP. Nevertheless, it's important to remember that your SWAG-GER-limiting beliefs originated to protect you. However misguided and detrimental they are to you now, they began with good intentions. If you recall, we discussed the power of gratitude in Chapter 5. Saying "thank you" is a way to demonstrate your gratitude for whatever help your SWAGGER-limiting beliefs may have provided to you over the years.

Additionally, by focusing on gratitude, you shift your energy from a negative trajectory to a positive one. This energy shift supports your ability to productively move forward.

Returning to our beleaguered tennis player, this step of the REP strategy might be something like this: "Thank you for showing up, but you're not helping me right now. I need you to leave so I can focus my energy on winning this match. I've been in worse situations before and somehow managed to make it through. I can do it again. What would have to be true for me to win this match?"

As an overall note on **REP**: for purposes of illustration and clarity, we've focused on each step separately. This could make the REP strategy seem more time-consuming than it actually is. Not unlike trying anything else for the first time, it might feel a bit cumbersome initially. However, the more you practice, the easier it will become and the more quickly you'll be able to move through the steps.

Before you know it, you'll be working through the REP steps with fluency and ease becoming more and more empowered with every repetition.

Owning Your Power

The time has come for you to apply what you've learned and finally take out that key and unlock the chains holding you back.

The word empowered means "having the knowledge, confidence, and skills to do things for yourself." As I said at the beginning of this chapter, you have everything you need to not only break free from these chains but unleash your potential and achieve what you once deemed impossible.

It's time to set yourself and your potential free. The activities included here are designed to help you get started uncovering and overcoming your SWAGGER-limiting beliefs. But now you can also find additional activities and daily reinforcements to support you on your journey at swaggeru. com/my_swagger.

All I can say is, "Watch out world because here you come!" I can't wait to see the wondrous things you create.

A Final Important Note

Please keep in mind that working to uncover your SWAGGER-limiting beliefs can elicit powerful memories and emotions. Don't hesitate to seek professional assistance to support your efforts in overcoming them.

Activity: Identifying Your SWAGGER-limiting Beliefs
Time: 20–30 minutes

Before you can overcome your SWAGGER-limiting beliefs, you must first be able to identify them. This activity is designed to help you take a closer look at the destructive beliefs holding you and your potential back.

Step 1
Think of all of the destructive conversations you've had with yourself over the years. Make a list of the SWAGGER-limiting beliefs you fall victim to most often.

Below is a sample list to get you started. If you have additional SWAGGER-limiting beliefs not listed here, record those as well.

- I can't because . . .
- I'm not good/smart/experienced, etc. enough.
- I'm too old/young, etc.
- Good things only happen to other people.
- I don't have time.
- I'm not worthy enough.

- Bad things always happen to me.
- People will judge me or think poorly of me.
- I don't deserve to be happy/loved/successful, etc.
- I'll never be successful/happy, etc.
- Sure, they can do it, but I'll never be able to.
- I'll never be good/smart/thin, etc. enough.
- If I can't do it perfectly/exceptionally well, then why bother?
- I'm a failure.
- I'll never be as good as them.
- I'm an idiot.
- I'm afraid I'll fail.
- This is my life, and I just have to accept it.
- I'm just waiting for the other shoe to drop, it always does.
- I'm not good at that.

Step 2

You made it. You're still here. Take a deep breath. Sit up nice and tall with a sense of strength and fortitude.

Now take a look at the list you've created and answer the following questions.

- What have these SWAGGER-limiting beliefs kept you from doing?
- What have you missed out on as a result of these SWAGGER-limiting beliefs?
- What might be possible if you stopped allowing these SWAGGER-limiting beliefs to get in your way?

Activity: Where Are You From?
Time: 30 minutes

Now that you've identified what some of your SWAGGER-limiting beliefs are, it's time to dig a bit deeper and learn about what caused them to start showing up in the first place.

This activity might bring some powerful memories and emotions to the surface, so make sure you're in a private location to complete it.

Step 1
Select two or three SWAGGER-limiting beliefs from your list. Record each one on a separate piece of paper or a blank page on your computer.

Step 2
Focusing on one at a time, complete the following for each SWAGGER-limiting belief, and record your thoughts:

- Think back through your life experiences and try to determine when this SWAGGER-limiting belief first started showing up.
- What do you think the SWAGGER-limiting belief was trying to protect you or save you from?
- Is this belief still valid? What evidence do you have to support this?
- How does this belief currently serve you and what you're working to achieve or accomplish?

Daily Reinforcement: Powers of Observation
Time: 5 minutes

To improve your ability to work through the REP winning strategy, it's important to strengthen your powers of observation. This reinforcement helps you become more aware of your feelings and physical reactions.

It's most beneficial when you do this reinforcement multiple times throughout the day.

Step 1
Take a moment and calm your thoughts by focusing on your breathing. On your inhale, say silently to yourself, "Inhale." On your exhale, say silently to yourself, "Exhale." Don't worry if your thoughts wander a little. Just bring your thoughts back to your breath. Do this for two minutes.

Step 2
With your eyes closed, begin at the top of your head, and start to scan how your body feels.

Do you notice any tension in your eyes? How does the skin feel on your face? Is it tight, or relaxed? Is your jaw clenched or slack?

Continue moving down the body until you've taken note of how your entire body feels at that moment.

Daily Reinforcement: REPs
Time: 5 minutes

Becoming better and more efficient working through the REP winning strategy requires practice.

Similar to a mock trial, this reinforcement gives you practice cycles working through the steps and works to build your confidence in the process.

Step 1
Select one of your SWAGGER-limiting beliefs to work with from your list. Now imagine that this SWAGGER-limiting belief has just arrived unannounced.

Step 2
Work through the **REP** winning strategy steps as follows and record your responses:

Recognize
- What feelings or physical reactions are present?
- What trigger caused this belief to show up?
- What thoughts and statements start to run through your head?

Evaluate
- What evidence exists to support or refute the claims of this belief?
- What does the worst-case scenario look like?
- Is this belief currently serving you and what you're working to accomplish?

Pivot
- Thank the belief for coming and then say, "Goodbye."
- What's a more constructive thought you can use to replace a destructive one?

 ## SWAGGER Insight

- Your SWAGGER-limiting beliefs are what keep you from tapping into what makes you unique and extraordinary, being your best self, performing at your best, and living your best life.
- SWAGGER-limiting beliefs don't care how wealthy, intelligent, or successful you are. They're not picky; they show up regardless.

- SWAGGER-limiting beliefs are uninvited guests. No one asked them to come to the party, but they showed up anyway, and we keep letting them in and allowing them to wreak havoc on our lives.
- There's no possible scenario in which we'd tolerate the kind of talk our SWAGGER-limiting beliefs say to us from anyone else.
- Your SWAGGER-limiting beliefs originated *to protect you* from pain and suffering.
- The intense emotions that you connect with your life experiences create powerful memories and, ultimately, directly influence your SWAGGER-limiting beliefs.
- Sometimes SWAGGER-limiting beliefs come from a person of authority or someone you look up to.
- SWAGGER-limiting beliefs are born out of fear. Fear of getting hurt, fear of failing, fear of being judged, and on and on and on.
- The more we trust in these SWAGGER-limiting beliefs and the more power we give to them, the more they control the trajectory of our lives.
- SWAGGER-limiting beliefs behave much like a Diminisher leader, as defined by Liz Wiseman in her book *Multipliers*. They diminish your ability to utilize your full potential and live your life at your highest capacity.
- SWAGGER-limiting beliefs work from a "fixed mindset" as described by Carol Dweck in her book *Mindset: The New Psychology of Success*. This mindset creates a tendency for you to be cautious and conservative.
- SWAGGER-limiting beliefs are sneaky and really good at getting you to believe what they're saying.
- SWAGGER-limiting beliefs act as saboteurs, as discussed by Shirzad Chamine in his book *Positive Intelligence*. They constantly work to undermine you at every turn.
- "Explanatory style" is the way in which you consistently explain to yourself why events happen.

- SWAGGER-limiting beliefs can be categorized as using a "pessimistic explanatory style," as defined by Martin Seligman in his book *Learned Optimism*. They place the blame squarely on your shoulders with a sense of pervasiveness and permanence.
- It doesn't matter whether you're an optimist or pessimist, your logical brain can be hijacked by these statements at any time.
- Consistently using a pessimistic explanatory style is a precursor to depression.
- The steady stream of destructive thoughts that your SWAGGER-limiting beliefs bring with them plant the seeds that foster helplessness.
- Seligman found that helplessness can be learned.
- "Learned helplessness" is when you quit and give up because you believe that there's nothing you can do to change your situation or circumstances.
- SWAGGER-limiting beliefs can cause significant damage to your self-worth—it's a death by a thousand cuts.
- Sustained damage to your self-worth can lead to severe depression, helplessness, even suicide.
- SWAGGER-limiting beliefs are like self-fulfilling prophecies which can jeopardize your performance and cause chaos in the rest of your life.
- Your SWAGGER-limiting beliefs continually encourage you to underutilize your potential, holding you back, putting you in your own way, and keeping you from fully stepping into who you're capable of being.
- The only reason your SWAGGER-limiting beliefs have power and control is because you keep inviting them in.
- What you believe is what you create, and what others see.
- Remember that your SWAGGER-limiting beliefs are just that. Beliefs. They aren't statements of facts. They aren't the truth.
- Your SWAGGER-limiting beliefs are nothing more than habits about the way you currently think of yourself and your circum-

stances. These habits don't have to last forever. They're not a fait accompli.

- You can choose the way you think.
- You can determine how you think about yourself, others, and your circumstances.
- You'll never be good enough and things won't change unless you change the way you think and what you say to yourself.
- Creating a shift in your thinking isn't so much about saying nice things to yourself, but rather about how you view the setbacks, the making mistakes, and the personal defeats as you progress forward.
- Once you shift the way you think, you can change the destructive things you say to yourself when faced with setbacks that inevitably happen.
- Experiences that previously appeared to be your fault, or had a sense of permanence, or seemed to impact all aspects of your life, are nothing more than opportunities for learning, growth, and development.
- Choosing to see things through an optimistic lens provides a more productive path forward, wherein you take ownership and control of what comes next.
- Taking ownership and control does mean that you can no longer blame others for the mistakes you make or your lot in life.
- Shifting the way you think will take **P to the Power of 3 – Patience – Practice –Perseverance**.
- The winning strategy to overcome your SWAGGER-limiting beliefs is **REP—R**ecognize, **E**valuate, and **P**ivot.
  - **Recognize** is about being vigilant and noticing when your SWAGGER-limiting beliefs show up.
  - **Evaluate** is about challenging your SWAGGER-limiting beliefs and using facts to refute them.
  - **Pivot** is about shifting your thoughts and what you say to yourself to enable you to move forward more productively.
- You have everything you need to break free from your SWAG-

GER-limiting beliefs, unleash your potential, and achieve what you once deemed impossible.

- Please keep in mind that working to uncover your SWAGGER-limiting beliefs can elicit powerful memories and emotions. Don't hesitate to seek professional assistance to support your efforts in overcoming them.

CHAPTER 8

Being Renewed Through Your Passion and Purpose

First of all, let me just say congratulations.

That last chapter was a doozie. Even writing it was incredibly difficult, so I can only imagine how challenging it was for you to read and work through it.

Nevertheless, you did. You made it. Way to go! Well done! Take a bow. Now, let's keep that momentum going.

But, first, a question. What information do you need to enter into your phone GPS to get to where you're headed?

The destination. Exactly.

What additional information is required to ensure your GPS can provide you with accurate directions to get you to your destination?

Your current location. That's right.

Okay, so you're ready to go. You've entered both the destination you want to go to and the current location you're at into your GPS, and you hit the start button for those step-by-step directions.

Then, you begin driving, guided by the pleasant, or annoying, automated voice from your phone. The voice calmly tells you where to turn, and also how much further you have to go before the next direction.

But then guess what? You just missed the turn you were supposed to take.

"Oops."

Well, maybe you use some word other than "oops," but you get the idea.

In any case, your GPS beeps at you to let you know that you made an error and missed your turn, then proceeds to re-route you, giving you new instructions. If you spectacularly messed up on your directions, then the GPS might even tell you to make a U-turn at the next light, but the beautiful thing is that no matter how many missteps you make, that GPS of yours will always figure out a way to get you back on track, and no matter what, you'll eventually reach your desired destination.

That's precisely what it's like when you have a clearly articulated purpose. When you're crystal clear on your purpose, you'll always be able to get back on track and heading in the right direction.

In this way, it acts just like a GPS. Only, in this case, instead of meaning "Global Positioning System," I like to think of it as the "Guided Purpose Support."

When you're guided by your purpose, you can stay on track and aligned regardless of what life throws at you. This GPS—Guided Purpose Support—is available and ready to help whenever you find yourself faced with decisions and choices to make.

You can ask yourself, "Is this in line with my purpose?" or "Does this help me live my purpose?" Asking these questions is like double-checking with the GPS to make sure that you're still moving in the right direction and haven't accidentally taken that wrong turn somewhere on the journey.

See, *purpose* is the last piece of the SWAGGER puzzle. Now, just because it's last, don't think that means it's any less significant. In fact, SWAGGER without purpose is like a rough diamond that has yet to be cut and polished. It'll never reach its magnificent potential until expert hands shape it to bring out its color, clarity, and brilliance.

It's the same with your SWAGGER. Remember, the **R** in SWAG-GER stands for **Renewed,** which is considered to mean to make new, or perhaps to become energized and invigorated. But you can't be renewed, and your SWAGGER can't reach its full potency and strength, without purpose. Your SWAGGER will be there, but it'll only be mediocre, not exceptional.

You didn't come this far for mediocre, did you? No, you're here to shoot for the stars, not settle for less than extraordinary.

Right about now, you might be thinking, "But I don't have a purpose. Or if I do, I have no idea what it is."

I can certainly appreciate why you might feel that way. But fear not, that's what this chapter is all about. Because believe it or not, you do have a purpose. You just haven't uncovered it yet. You might not even have a fully developed purpose by the end of this chapter, but you'll be well on your way to figuring it out.

So what do you say? Are you ready to get started? Are you ready to start honing and polishing your SWAGGER to bring out its magnificence?

Fantastic!

Now, before we tackle how to uncover your purpose, let's first explore more about what purpose is, why it's such an essential part of claiming your SWAGGER, and the role passion plays in honing your purpose.

"Who," "What," and, oh yeah, "Why"

Sometimes to better understand one concept it's helpful to define it in the context of others. In my work with global leaders, there was often confusion about the words "mission," "vision," "values," and "purpose."

Now, we already learned in Chapter 6 that company *values* tell us who they are and how they behave.

But what about those other three?

These common words get thrown around and are frequently used interchangeably and incorrectly There are important distinctions between these words that make each one unique. So let's take a look at all of them to gain clarity around purpose.

A *mission* statement shares what the company does and who they serve. For example, Starbucks's mission is, "To inspire and nurture the human spirit—one person, one cup, and one neighborhood at a time." So this statement tells us what the company does: inspire and nurture the human spirit, in this case, by serving coffee, other beverages, and food, in a welcoming environment. It also lets us know who they serve: the people and neighborhoods.

A *vision* statement shares what the company would like to achieve or accomplish in the future. It's an aspirational statement that describes a future state for the organization. An example of this is Disney's vision, "To be one of the world's leading producers and providers of entertainment and information." This statement describes Disney's desire to be a world leader in the area of entertainment and information.

See the difference? Mission statements emphasize what is being done here and now, while vision statements focus on a specific ambition or goal for the future.

So what about purpose? What does a company's *purpose* tell us?

Below is a list of organizational *purpose* statements. Read through the list and see if you can identify the company each belongs to.

Your first instinct might be to look these up on the Internet. But where's the fun in that? Think of this as a challenge and make your guesses before you read the next paragraph.

- *"Discovering the value of 'real' beauty and improving self-esteem worldwide."*
- *"Better care for a better world."*
- *"To inspire and develop children to think creatively, reason systematically, and release their potential to shape their own future—experiencing the endless human possibility."*

What did you come up with?

Let's work through them together. The first one is the purpose statement for Dove, a Unilever brand. They have a strong desire to change the way people see beauty. You've likely seen the soap and advertisements for their "Self-Esteem" campaign.

The second statement is how Kimberly-Clark defines its purpose. Kimberly-Clark is a multinational personal care corporation that produces paper-based consumer products. You might be familiar with some of their brands, like Cottonelle, Kleenex, or Huggies.

The third one is the purpose statement for Lego, the Danish toy production company. Even if you don't have kids, you can be a Lego devotee, addicted to building intricate sets like a Ferrari or the Taj Mahal.

So what did you notice about these *purpose* statements in contrast with *mission* and *vision* statements?

If the mission tells us what a company does and who they serve, and the vision tells us what they'd like to become or achieve, what's left?

Precisely—why. Why the company exists. A company's purpose tells us why they exist in the first place.

Now, you might have noticed some parallels between Starbucks's mission statement and Lego's purpose statement. They both use the words "to inspire" and appear on the surface to be similar. Upon closer examination, however, we can spot a clear difference. One of the key aspects that separates a company's purpose from its mission is the outcome. In the purpose statement for Lego, the outcome is "to enable children to shape their own future and experience endless human possibility." The mission statement for Starbucks doesn't express an outcome. It doesn't say anything about why they'd like to inspire and nurture the human spirit. That's what makes it a mission instead of a purpose.

Another thing to highlight is the aim of the outcome. It's usually focused on something that impacts the greater good; something bigger than profits or company growth. The outcome is outward-looking, not inward-looking.

Check out the impacts of the other two purpose statements listed above. The impact of Dove's purpose is to "improve self-esteem worldwide." For Kimberly-Clark, it's "to help create or foster a better world." Both of these outcomes are quite large in scope and aim to positively impact humanity and the world as a whole.

Let's recap and pull this all together.

A *purpose* describes why a company exists and includes an outcome that's focused on positively impacting the greater good.

Is this all starting to make more sense now?

You can also look at it this way: maybe you're familiar with the term "tapping into hearts and minds." Well, the mission and vision connect with the mind. They communicate with the logical brain. They tell you what the company does, who they serve, and what they desire to achieve or become in the future. However, those are just facts and information. They don't really move you.

So purpose is what connects to people's hearts. It's what more and more companies are using to inspire their employees, differentiate themselves from their competition, and connect more deeply with their customers and clients.

That's exactly what best-selling author and visionary thinker Simon Sinek delineated in his book *Start with Why*.

He summed up the concept like this: "People don't buy what you do; they buy why you do it."

As humans, we're constantly searching for meaning and have a deep desire to connect with and be part of something bigger than ourselves. Purpose provides this. When you buy from that company, you buy into and, by proxy, become part of their "why."

In his book *Drive*, best-selling author Daniel Pink talks about the three most critical intrinsic motivators of human performance, one of which is purpose.

Keynote speaker and author Zach Mercurio writes in his book, *The Invisible Leader*, "Results don't drive people, purpose does."

Okay, so now let's take this from an organizational perspective to a personal one.

Instead of describing why a company exists, your *purpose* would describe why you exist, including how you'd like to contribute to the greater good. It would help define your "why"—your reason for being and the part you play in positively impacting the world around you. Your purpose is what drives you and keeps you going even when things get tough.

When you're wholeheartedly driven by your purpose, nothing and no one will be able to get in your way of accomplishing what you set out to do. It won't matter how many obstacles are placed in your path because living your purpose is much bigger than you. It's not about *you* succeeding, it's about the positive impact *you* can have on *others*. True purpose is living in service of others. That's what makes it so powerful.

You've probably heard this story or something like it before. Nevertheless, it's worth repeating, so bear with me as I tell it again.

A woman walks by a person at a construction site and asks them what they're doing. They flatly reply, "I'm laying bricks." She sees another person working and asks them what they're doing. They smile and say, "I'm building a wall." She walks by yet one more individual on the site and asks them what they're doing. They excitedly exclaim, "I'm building a hospital!"

All of the people she encountered on the construction site were performing the exact same task. So why the varied responses?

The difference comes from the meaning they assigned to their work and the purpose they found in their everyday life.

The first person she came across at the site saw their job from a narrow perspective. They could only see the obvious basic facts—the act of laying bricks. The second person visualized their role from a slightly different point of view. Why do you lay bricks? Well, to build a wall of course. The third person saw even more than this. They recognized that they weren't merely laying bricks or building a wall. The work they were doing when completed would serve the whole community and help people have access to life-saving medical care. They'd uncovered a purpose much bigger than themselves.

So which person do you think was more excited to get up and go to work every day? Precisely! The person who'd found purpose and meaning in their job.

Purpose is inspiring, energizing, and dare I say, transformative.

When you're renewed by your purpose, it's as if you're finally awakened and brought to life. Purpose is the difference between merely surviving your life and thriving in it.

But what happens when your purpose remains hidden and undiscovered?

How Did I Get Here?

If you saw the movie *Forrest Gump*, you probably remember the part where he goes for a run with no real destination in mind.

Forrest ends up getting to the edge of his town and just decides to keep going. He proceeds to run across Alabama and continues running until he reaches the coast. Then "for no particular reason" he keeps going and determines that since he made it this far, he might as well turn around and head to the other coast. He ends up running across the country multiple times.

Many people can't fathom the idea that Forrest was simply running for the heck of it. It made no sense to them. "No," they think, "he must be running for some cause, like to fight hunger or for world peace."

But he just kept replying, "I just felt like running."

Ever wake up in the morning and wonder, "How in the world did I get here?"

Yeah, me too. When I was traveling internationally a lot for work, there were so many times that I'd wake up in the middle of the night and not recognize my surroundings. I'd have absolutely no idea where I was. It would be a bit startling at first and usually took a few minutes to gather myself and think about where I'd been so I could figure out where I was. It's not a sensation I care to repeat, and I don't recommend it to anyone.

However, this is exactly what it's like when you don't have purpose to guide you. Similar to Forrest running across the country, or me waking up in the middle of the night, without purpose, you have no idea of where you're going, and when you arrive somewhere, you likely have no clue as to how you got there.

This quote, which is attributed to the Cheshire Cat from *Alice in Wonderland*, sums it up beautifully: "If you don't know where you're going, any road will get you there."

Going through life without a purpose as your guide makes you like a hamster on a wheel, and you just keep running and running, but somehow remain unfulfilled and unsatisfied. No matter what choice you make, or what road you take, nothing seems to fill the void. You still always feel empty.

This often creates the "I'll Be Happy When" syndrome. You know, "I'll be happy when *I graduate*, or when *I get married*, or when *I get the job*, or when *I have kids*, or when *I get a promotion*." When this syndrome is in effect, you just keep unsuccessfully trying to fill the emptiness, hoping that the next milestone is the one.

But what's really missing doesn't come from the outside, it comes from the inside. It comes from uncovering your purpose and bringing it into the light, and when you allow your purpose to remain hidden, you're inviting danger and risk into your life. You're vulnerable to the influences of external forces.

Your innate desire to find meaning, see, to be part of something that matters, is still aching to be satisfied. If it doesn't come from your purpose, you'll seek to fulfill it through other avenues. This could lead you down unhealthy and destructive paths, like addiction, indoctrination, even suicide.

Have you ever wondered why some people turn to alcohol, drugs, sex, and other addictions?

It's because they're seeking the release it provides. For a brief moment, they're freed from their emptiness. They believe they've found happiness, albeit fleeting, and continue to chase the high they achieve through the addiction.

Why might people join cults or become part of radical organizations? It's because they're searching for meaning and have a need to be part of something bigger than themselves. By joining, they believe they're helping to further a noble cause, and by succumbing to indoctrination, they thus artificially appease their longing.

What could drive people to think suicide is an option? One possibility is that they've found their life to be devoid of meaning, and therefore, not worth living. If there's no reason for being, then why continue? Through suicide, they aim to permanently put themselves out of their desolation.

I'm sorry, I know you thought we'd left these unsavory topics in the last chapter. Now, obviously, there could be many reasons why people might turn down the paths toward addiction, indoctrination, or suicide. But I'd be remiss if I didn't call out the connection all of those have to a lack of purpose.

Remember, uncovering your purpose isn't a nice asset to have, it's an essential component for your overall well-being and happiness.

Without purpose, your SWAGGER can't shine, and you can't thrive. You just become one of the millions of unhappy and unfulfilled people wandering aimlessly, or flitting from one thing to the next, trying to get through life.

A great example of this comes from the movie *City Slickers*.

Billy Crystal plays a character named Mitch who's having what some might call a mid-life crisis. I tend to call this a "purpose crisis." He has a wonderful wife, a loving family, and a great job that he's incredibly good at. You'd think Mitch had it all. Yet he wakes up each day just wondering what it's all about. His smile has vanished, as has his joy and zest for life. He's lost and searching for meaning. He finds himself struggling through each day, just to get up and do it all over again.

This might sound familiar.

During a cattle drive with his two longtime friends, Mitch comes across a weathered old cowboy who seems to have figured out the secret to life. Following several mishaps and catastrophes that take place during their adventure, Mitch finds his purpose—his "one thing." His reason for being. Then he emerges from the experience renewed, refreshed, and reinvigorated. We're never told what that "one thing" turns out to be, but that's because it's different for everyone. Just as I can't tell you what your purpose is, only you can determine that. However, what you do notice in the movie is the dramatic shift in the joy, fulfillment, and sheer delight the character Mitch now has for life, because he found his purpose.

Let's look at one more example.

I'm sure you're familiar with the classic holiday story by Charles Dickens, *A Christmas Carol*. There are numerous versions of the tale, and it's beloved by many. I know in our household we simply won't have Christmas without watching *The Muppet Christmas Carol*. In any case, regardless of which one you choose, the main premise stays the same, and it's a wonderful illustration of what happens when people have a misguided purpose.

The lead character, Ebenezer Scrooge, wrongly believes that he's found his purpose and is living it each day to the fullest. But his misguided purpose is more like an obsession: he aims to amass as much money as he possibly can and doesn't care who he hurts in the process. The problem with this plan is that Scrooge is utterly miserable and alone. The meaning he envisions as his secret to life continues to leave him unsatisfied, empty, and devoid of feeling. It doesn't matter how much money he acquires, nothing seems to be able to fill the void inside.

In a stroke of luck, Scrooge is visited by three spirits who help to open his heart and awaken his soul. The journeys through the past, present, and future enable him to find new meaning in his life and his true purpose. When Scrooge rises the following morning after his harrowing adventure, he's as "giddy as a schoolboy." He's full of excitement and wonder. He runs around in circles, unable to contain his enthusiasm, and can't figure out what to do first. He has literally been transformed by his newfound purpose.

In each of these examples, the main character was trudging through life, unhappy and unfulfilled. Their purpose remained hidden—locked away, and out of view. Transformation and renewal only took place once they uncovered that purpose and brought it into the light.

So what about you? Are you happy with where you are today? Are you merely surviving, like the characters we highlighted?

Don't worry if you are because I was too. But, lucky for you, finding and awakening your purpose doesn't require a cattle drive or being visited by spirits in the middle of the night.

I'm sure some thoughts going through your mind at the moment might be, "Okay, great Jennifer, so how do I go about finding it then?"

Well, a good place to start is by focusing on your passion.

The Power of Passion

I grew up in a military family. We moved every two to four years. One of the places where we lived was Fayetteville, North Carolina. Our house was right across the street from a lake. I used to love sitting on the front porch and watching the thunderstorms over the water. I was fascinated by the lightning and how it would illuminate the whole sky. It was quite a spectacle—like Mother Nature's fireworks.

Passion is much like lightning. When you find what you're passionate about, it's as if the energy can't be contained and must find a release.

Mother Nature must've been paying attention to me just now, because there's a thunderstorm taking place as I write this—what a coincidence.

Passion is considered having strong and barely controllable emotions. When you do something you're passionate about, the joy and pleasure you experience are difficult to contain. That's why it's called a *passion*.

If you listed your passions right now, what would they be? Do give that question some thought, but don't answer it just yet.

You can be passionate about a lot of things, and life is entirely more enjoyable when you're actively participating in your passions.

As an example, for me, passions would be food, travel, my horses, and fly fishing, just to name a few. If my husband and I aren't going on a fishing trip and he asks me what I'd like to do on a vacation, I usually say, "Eat, drink, and shop," not necessarily in that order.

Food is unquestionably one of my greatest passions. I love cooking and experimenting with flavors. My husband calls me "flavor obsessed."

Although I guess I'm what you would call a self-trained chef, I've taught cooking classes at Sur La Table and in our home kitchen when we lived in Arizona. I'm one of those people who typically cooks without recipes, focusing on taste and a balance of flavors. If I do use recipes, they're merely a starting point or a catalyst for ideas. Everything I make has a bit of my signature spin on it.

If you had to categorize my cooking, you'd probably call it "fusion." That's because I tend to combine flavors and spices from different regional and ethnic cuisines to create my own version of a dish. In case you were wondering, yes, a cookbook by me has been highly requested from both family and friends. So don't worry, that's in the works for a future publication.

The greatest pleasure I receive from cooking is watching other people enjoy the food I've prepared. Seeing their eyes close with ecstasy is so gratifying (and yes, you read that right). In fact, I believe that you can experience what I call a "food orgasm." It's that moment when you're completely transported from reality and immersed in the flavors caressing your tongue.

Now, as I said, food is just one of my passions, and it's important to point out that passions can be fleeting; they can shift and change throughout your life. However, those passions are still what will help lead you to your purpose. Sometimes events will take place in life that help awaken new passions. Those passions will then lead you closer to uncovering your purpose. This is when magic happens and sparks begin to fly. It might not feel that way when you're initially experiencing these moments, nevertheless, once you've made it through and you're able to reflect, you recognize the significance and wonder of it. When you align your passion with your purpose, it acts like a turbocharger. If you're a fan of *Star Wars*, it's like making the jump to lightspeed.

Let's take a look at two stories that bring this idea to life.

Malala Yousafzai was born in Pakistan, where her father was a teacher and ran a school for girls in their village. The Taliban gained control of the region when she was only 11 years old and banned many things, including girls going to school.

Enraged by the idea that girls weren't allowed to go to school, Malala began standing up for girls everywhere and speaking publicly about the right to learn. She had found her passion: helping girls everywhere have access to a good and safe education. For this, however, she also became a target, and at the age of fifteen, she was shot in the head by a masked gunman while riding a bus.

When Malala woke up in England after surviving the assassination attempt, she was more determined than ever. It was as if instead of extinguishing her flame, the gunman had poured gasoline on her fire. In that fateful moment, Malala became more resolute in her passion, and this immediately illuminated her purpose.

Following months of surgeries and rehabilitation, and with the help of her father, Malala established The Malala Fund. This charity exists for the sole purpose of ensuring that every girl has the opportunity to learn and lead so they can create the future of their choosing. In 2014, Malala was awarded the Nobel Peace Prize for her efforts. She graduated from Oxford University in 2020, and today, along with many talented team members across the globe, she continues the fight to build a brighter future for girls everywhere.

This next story is a personal one. Although I didn't win a Nobel Peace Prize or graduate from Oxford, the story is no less powerful.

My husband and I were married in Scotland. It was a small ceremony with just immediate family present. It was absolutely beautiful.

While in Scotland the week leading up to the wedding, my husband became ill. We thought it was just a common cold or a respiratory issue caused by allergies. So we carried on with our plans and preparations for the wedding. The big day arrived, and my husband was still ill, although he masked it well. "Mind over matter," as they say. He made it through the ceremony and the family events planned for the following day.

However, I could see that he was getting worse instead of better.

We had planned a nice, long honeymoon that was going to consist of touring all over the country. But as we were making our way up the stairs to our room on our first of many stops, it became clear that my husband's condition had significantly worsened. He couldn't even walk up the stairs. His breathing was shallow, and he couldn't catch his breath.

Now, my husband had been a runner all his life, so the fact that he couldn't walk up the stairs without getting winded was a huge sign, and not a good one. We attempted to see a doctor at the local health facility, but since we weren't part of the medical system in Scotland, we were denied access and couldn't be seen. So that evening, we faced a hard truth. The circumstances were dire, and we needed to get him back home so that he could get the medical attention he needed. I spent the entire night on the phone trying, in many cases unsuccessfully, to cancel the remainder of the honeymoon, and I also had to perform the miraculous feat of rebooking a flight home from Europe in the middle of summer.

Somehow, I managed to get us rebooked, and after another sleepless night of watching to make sure my husband was still breathing, we finally made it on our way home.

At that point, it's important to note that I hadn't slept in two days, but I still couldn't close my eyes. I knew we weren't out of the woods yet, and, frankly, I was afraid that he might stop breathing at any moment.

We arrived home, cleaned up, and rushed him over to the emergency room at the Arizona Mayo Clinic.

They admitted him immediately.

It turned out, my husband had 100 percent pneumonia in both lungs. They said that if we hadn't shown up when we did, he would likely have passed away within days. He was placed in an isolation room since we'd come from overseas and they'd yet to identify what he was suffering from. During this entire ordeal, my husband kept telling me that he'd be okay if this was the end. He'd lived a good life and was happy, he said. He was at peace.

What? I screamed in my mind.

"Well, I'm glad you're okay with this," I said to myself, "but I'm not! We're supposed to be starting this part of our life together—not ending it!"

Using humor as I often do during stressful times, I joked with him. "So you had to test out the whole 'in sickness and in health' thing right away, huh? You couldn't have waited a little longer to do that?"

Ultimately, my husband was diagnosed with a condition called valley fever. It's caused by a fungus found in the soil. You see, we'd been in the process of renovating our house prior to departing for the wedding, and he'd just finished removing some ornamental orange trees from our backyard that hadn't been disturbed for many years. Apparently, he'd inhaled the spores, and they'd infected his lungs.

While it sounds scary—and it was, by the way—it was also very treatable. In case you're wondering, he did make a full recovery.

Before we had gotten married, my husband gave me an amazing gift: the opportunity to figure out what I wanted to do with my life. Or, you might say, what I wanted to be when I grew up. What he offered me was priceless. He gave me the flexibility and time to explore and uncover my purpose in life. Well, with his near-death experience, coupled with the passing of my sister only a few years before, I became more determined than ever not to squander this precious gift that I'd been given. This life-shaping moment reinforced the idea that life is short and should be lived to the fullest.

When you're faced with how fleeting life is, the time you do spend on earth begins to take on new importance. I knew that I wanted to leave this world a better place than when I'd entered it, which meant to me at that moment that I needed to get clear on how I was going to make my mark.

I used this traumatic experience to specifically, define, and articulate my passion, and I worked through many iterations before I'd boiled it down to fifteen words or less. I then envisioned and recorded what it looked like when I was living that passion.

Below is what I wrote.

Passion: To help millions of people create positive and sustainable change in their lives.

When I'm living my passion:
- I'm using my talents and expertise to help others.
- I have a global impact.
- I speak to large groups.
- I'm well respected and highly regarded for the work I do.
- I have a superbly talented, creative, and supportive team to work with.
- I'm continually stimulated and encouraged to grow.
- I wake up every morning excited to do my work.
- I'm loving my life and having fun in all that I do.

Generating such granularity enabled me to seek out opportunities where I could live this passion daily. Homing in on this passion is what led me to my role in global leadership development, and ultimately to uncovering my true purpose, which I'll share with you in a bit. This is what I mean by the power of passion and how it can guide you to your purpose.

If you're thinking right now that you don't have the luxury of finding your passion and purpose, think again. Don't be misled by these stories. You don't have to stop everything or change what you do to uncover your passion and purpose and live them daily. Even if you're just trying to do anything to put food on the table and keep a roof over your head, you can do this.

So now, before we continue, breathe a bit easier, my friend. You've got this. Let's explore what's involved in uncovering your purpose.

The Art and Science of Purpose

Cooking necessitates a combination of both art and science. Artful masterpieces are fashioned by experimenting with ingredients until you've found just the right balance of flavors. When creating a new recipe, you rarely get it right the first time around. It's only through trial and error that you identify what's needed to take a dish from good to exceptional.

This is similar to uncovering your purpose. It requires experimentation, analysis, and trial and error to bring your purpose to life. Just remember **P to the Power of 3 – Patience – Practice – Perseverance**. You're not likely to hit a home run your first time at bat. You'll probably go through many iterations until you land on the purpose that truly resonates with you.

Another way that uncovering your purpose mimics the art and science of cooking rests with ingredients.

With cooking, two people can take the same ingredients and make completely different dishes. For example, they might be asked to make a pasta dish using a protein source, vegetables, and a sauce. There are numerous combinations they could come up with using those ingredients and you'd expect no two dishes to turn out the same. Perhaps one person uses a penne pasta and combines it with hot sausage and broccolini in a white wine sauce. Another uses capellini pasta with pancetta, red peppers, and onions in a fresh tomato sauce. Each dish is unique because of the specific ingredients used. The possibilities are endless.

Uncovering your purpose is the same. The categories of ingredients that help you formulate your purpose are common for everyone. However, your purpose is unique to you because the ingredients used are unique to you. This makes it statistically unlikely that two people will ever share an identical purpose.

Let me show you what I mean.

Most great recipes begin with a list of the ingredients you need to create the desired dish. In this case, the ingredients you need to discover your purpose are listed below. Many of these will seem familiar to you and that's one of the reasons why purpose comes at this stage in your SWAG-GER journey. The self-discovery work you've already accomplished has prepared you for this very moment.

Ingredients:
- Your passions—what you love doing most
- Your life experiences—the pivotal moments that influenced your passions
- Your strengths—what you're naturally good at
- Your core values—what matters most to you

Everyone possesses these ingredients. But no two people have the same passions, life experiences, strengths, or core values.

Consequently, no one will have the same purpose as you. Your purpose is as unique to you as are the ingredients you used to create it.

Okay, now it's time to put on your chef coat, roll up your sleeves, and get to work.

To uncover your purpose, you'll need to work through the "Purpose Recipe." You'll combine, question, experiment, and explore using the ingredients listed above to create your masterpiece.

Don't panic. Even if you're not comfortable in the kitchen, you'll be able to work through the recipe. All you have to do is follow the steps and get incredibly comfortable with asking questions.

So what do you say? Should we jump in?

The Purpose Recipe

Preparing Your Ingredients

Before you can successfully execute any recipe, you must first prepare your ingredients. This is often called *mise en place*, a French term that when translated means "putting in place" or "setting up." It's when chefs rinse, chop, slice, mince, or measure all of the ingredients they need and place them into small individual bowls so they're ready for the next steps. If you've watched any cooking shows or had dinner at a restaurant with an open kitchen, then you've probably seen this in action.

This recipe is no different; you have to gather and prepare your ingredients. Let's tackle the ingredient that requires the most work first.

Step 1: List your passions.

Start by listing your passions—what you love doing most of all.

For example, you might love coaching, volunteering, painting, music, traveling, solving problems, developing people, or building careers. Like flashes of lightning, your passions are what bring you uncontainable joy, energy, and enthusiasm.

Step 2: Craft a passion statement.

For each passion listed, craft a statement that clearly articulates or describes that passion using fifteen words or less.

To illustrate this, let's look at my passion for food and cooking as well as helping others. When these are described in a statement, they read like this.

- To nourish the soul and awaken the spirit through food and flavor.
- To help millions of people create positive and sustainable change in their lives.

This is harder than it looks, but you're not after perfection here. This is nothing more than an experiment meant to help you gain clarity around your passions.

To support this effort, begin by asking yourself the following questions: "What is it about this activity/experience that really excites and energizes me?" and/or "Why am I passionate about this?" This is actually a great time to channel your inner child and *keep* asking questions.

When my sister was younger, we used to call her "Miss Why" because she would always ask, "But why?" This small but significant three-letter word can help you dig deeper until you find the meaning behind your passions.

Ever heard of "The Five Whys"? It's often used in root cause analysis to help uncover what's at the heart of a problem or situation. You've likely seen or used this technique before. You follow each answer with the question why until you get to the real underlying issue.

So for every answer you give, keep asking yourself "Why?" until you feel confident you've revealed what sits at the core of your passions—something more meaningful than "because it's fun" or "because I like it." However, there's no need to overanalyze or get caught up in analysis paralysis. Just use this tool to support your efforts and have some fun with this exploration.

Step 3: Highlight your life experiences.

So now let's turn to the next ingredient in the recipe—your life experiences.

Make a list of the pivotal moments in your life that contributed to or influenced your passions. What you're looking for are those moments when you saw sparks or flashes of light because of the energy of the experience. You could call these your "lightning moments." For instance, the many joyful hours I spent in the kitchen as a child undoubtedly planted the seed for my passion for food and cooking. In preparing holiday meals, my sisters and I each had a role to play. My job was to bake the pies and cheesecakes. This seed that was planted as a child began to take root when I lived in San Francisco and experienced amazing flavors. That was the beginning of my lifelong love affair with food.

There are numerous life experiences connected to my passion for helping others. I've already described some, such as my "privilege of the platform" moment that I described in Chapter 3, which took place when I was teaching group fitness in college. Another experience that I've previously shared was when I delivered my first presentation in front of a large live audience without any slides to back me up.

There are so many more that I could call out, but you get the idea.

Step 4: List your strengths and core values.

Your strengths and core values are the easiest ingredients to prepare because you've already done the hard work of identifying them in Chapters 4 and 6. All you have to do here is list them. This will ensure that you can easily access them for the following steps in the recipe.

To continue using me as an example, I've listed mine below.

My strengths:
- Maximizer®
- Relator®
- Strategic®
- Individualization®
- Achiever®

My core values:
- Respect
- Honesty
- Integrity
- Pleasure
- Learning

Combine Your Ingredients

Now that you've prepared your ingredients, it's time to combine them.

As a chef, this is where you get to experiment and determine what ingredients work well together. Typically, you begin with your main ingredient and then add supplemental ingredients to come up with different combinations.

In this case, your main ingredient will be your passions.

Step 1: Select a passion to focus on.

You might have identified several things that you're passionate about. However, for these next steps, you'll need to focus on one passion at a time. I've identified two passions: my passion for food and cooking and my passion for helping others.

For this example, let's focus on my passion for helping others:

- To help millions of people create positive and sustainable change in their lives.

Step 2: Connect with your strengths.

In preparing your ingredients, you've already identified some life experiences that connect with this passion. So, in this step, you're working to determine how your strengths enable you to live your passion.

For example, my Maximizer® strength enables me to educate and inspire people to get the most out of themselves and their lives. My Relator® strength helps me develop strong relationships with the people I coach, support, or engage with. With my strength of individualization®, I'm able to help others discover what makes them unique and extraordinary. My Strategic® strength supports me in finding new paths and approaches to helping others. Finally, my Achiever® strength keeps me focused and on task, making sure to complete the goals I've set in living this passion.

Step 3: Align with your values.

This step is all about identifying how your passion aligns with your values.

Continuing with our example, my passion for helping others aligns with my values in the following ways:

- Respect—I respect people's uniqueness, differences, beliefs, and values.
- Honesty—Everything I do, create, and develop is with the utmost honesty and integrity.
- Pleasure—Not only do I derive pleasure from living this passion, but I also aim to encourage others to find and create pleasure in their lives.
- Learning—I'm constantly seeking to find new ways to foster learning in others.

Prepare Serving Recommendations

One of the things a chef does when creating a new recipe is prepare serving recommendations. Some of these might include serving size, how many people the recipe will serve, or what might be a good complement to the dish, such as whipped cream or a sprig of mint for garnish.

In this part of the "Purpose Recipe," your goal is to identify how you can serve others with this passion. As we mentioned earlier in the chapter, true purpose is always in service of others. That's where its power lies. So to help you move closer to uncovering your purpose, it's helpful to imagine the many ways you might be able to serve others.

Step 1: Ideate

In this step, we'll employ a technique that's often used when innovating, called *ideation*. The objective of this technique is to come up with as many ideas as possible in a short amount of time.

It's like brainstorming. For example, you might see how many ideas you produce in five or ten minutes.

Most importantly, this is a no-judgment zone. Ideation isn't the place for judging or critiquing ideas. Its sole focus is on generating. This is the time to go crazy and have fun. Questions such as "What if?" and "How might I . . .?" are always great thought starters. You'll want to think about both the "who" and "how." As in, "Who can you serve, and how can you serve them?"

Let's play this out using my example of helping others create positive and sustainable change in their lives.

There are an endless number of ideas you can think of for who I could serve and how I could serve them with this passion. Below are just a few to provide a sample of what I mean.

- Children
- Teenagers
- Cancer survivors
- Adults in specific age groups

Okay, that's some of who I could serve. So what about how?

- I could help children develop fitness and health habits.
- I could help teenagers build self-esteem.
- I could help cancer survivors learn to see cancer as the spark that creates the rest of their life instead of as something they survive.
- I could help people discover what makes them unique and extraordinary.

Step 2: Choose your idea.

Now that you've generated your ideas for who you can serve and how you can serve them, it's time to choose the idea that you'll use to move forward with.

A best practice when innovating is to choose the most desirable idea. In this case, it's about choosing the idea that you get most excited about. Which idea gives you energy just by thinking about it?

For me, the idea that stands out and gives me the most energy is unquestionably helping people discover what makes them unique and extraordinary. My brain immediately starts to envision a plethora of opportunities surrounding this idea. For lack of a better way of describing it, it just feels right. I even get a fleeting moment when I say to myself, "This is what I'm meant to be doing."

Mix It All Together

Let's say you're a chef who's created a cookbook. You've spent countless hours meticulously crafting and testing recipes, and you're finally ready to pull it all together. Now comes the almost impossible task of naming the cookbook. How can you possibly distill everything that's included within into one name?

This is very much what it feels like to try and craft your purpose.

Think about it. You're attempting to describe why you exist, and somehow fit it into one sentence.

How crazy is that? It is crazy.

Nevertheless, when you're finally able to articulate your reason for being, it's one of the most influential and impactful things you can do for yourself.

Step 1: Combine your passion with service.

This step is like putting together the pieces of a puzzle. You have two separate pieces of information that you're working to bring together as one.

In this case, you're combining your passion statement with the idea you came up with for who you can serve and how you can serve them. Let's look at my example.

Passion statement:
* *To help millions of people create positive and sustainable change in their lives*

Who and how I can serve:
* *To help people discover what makes them unique and extraordinary*

If I combine these it might look something like this:
* *To help millions of people create positive and sustainable change in their lives by discovering what makes them unique and extraordinary*

Step 2: Determine your outcome

Okay, so it's still a bit clunky, but we're getting somewhere.

Now it's time to determine the outcome. As highlighted earlier in the chapter, an outcome is an essential component of a purpose statement. It's usually focused on something that impacts the greater good and is outward-looking not inward-looking.

Let's play with our example a bit. Perhaps we just need to adjust what we already have. The outcome of my purpose could look like this:

To help people create positive and sustainable
change in their lives and the world around them

Step 3: Draft your purpose.

You now have all the parts required to create a draft of your purpose. All that's left to do is create multiple versions and iterate until you land on one that resonates with you.

Once you get to that point, put it away. Come back to it a few days later and see if it still feels right. Additionally, you can share it with other people who know you well and see how they respond to it. This process may take some time, so again, I encourage you to be patient and give it the time it deserves.

Use the following format when crafting your purpose:

> *To _____(do what and for whom)_____ in order that, or so that _____(outcome) _____.*

A draft of my purpose statement might read as follows:

> *To help people discover what makes them unique and extraordinary so they can create positive and sustainable change in themselves and the world around them.*

After many iterations, my purpose now looks like this:

> *To ignite people's SWAGGER so they can transform their lives and the world around them.*

Step 4: Live your purpose.

It's not enough just to craft the statement. You also need to envision what it looks like when you're living your purpose.

What will it feel like, what will you be doing, and how will you know that you're living your purpose?

The more specific and granular you can be, the more likely you are to find and create ways to bring your purpose to life.

To craft descriptions of what it looks like to live your purpose, always use the present tense, such as "I am" and "I have," as if you're already doing what you're writing about.

Because passion and purpose are so closely linked, you'll find many similarities between the examples below and the ones I shared earlier in the chapter about living my passion.

- I'm living with SWAGGER.
- I'm using my talents and expertise to create a global SWAGGER movement.
- The world is better and brighter because of the SWAGGER movement.
- My words and my work have a global impact on millions of people.
- I spread the SWAGGER message by speaking and engaging with large groups.
- I'm well respected and highly regarded for the work I do.
- I have a superbly talented, creative, and supportive team to work with.
- I'm continually stimulated and encouraged to grow.
- I wake up every morning excited to do my work.
- I'm loving my life and having fun in all that I do.

When you embody your purpose, you're able to quench your search for meaning and desire to be part of something bigger than you.

You become renewed and rejuvenated.

Your SWAGGER realizes its full potential, enabling you to live with unimaginable joy and fulfillment.

Now It's Your Turn

Okay, I know that seems like a lot, and it is.

But this is your purpose we're talking about. This isn't something that can be boiled down into a couple of short steps. Your reason for being warrants a bit more time and thought.

My recommendation is to work through the Purpose Recipe. Focus on Part 1 first, and take your time moving through the steps.

Then, when you're ready for more, tackle Part 2. When you feel up for it, move on to Part 3.

Finally, when your mind is rested and the creative juices are flowing, complete Part 4. Breaking this into bite-sized pieces makes the work more manageable and doable.

Whatever you do, don't allow yourself to be overwhelmed and neglect to finish this part of claiming your SWAGGER. That would be like getting to the final mile in a marathon and giving up. Yes, you still have work to do, but if you give up now, everything you've done up to this point will be for nothing. All of the time and energy you've put in, not to mention the training and sacrifice it took to get to the starting line in the first place, will be wasted.

The finish line is in sight, my friend. This is the time to dig deep and gut it out. You've got this! Don't you dare give up now.

So what do you say, are you ready to start putting this learning into practice?

I thought so.

Activity: The Purpose Recipe Part 1, Prepare Your Ingredients
Time: 30–45 minutes

This activity is all about getting your ingredients prepared so that you can work through the remaining parts of the Purpose Recipe.

Step 1: List your passions
Make a list of your passions: what you love doing most of all.
For example, you might love coaching, volunteering, painting, music, traveling, solving problems, developing people, building careers.

Like flashes of lightning, your passions are what bring you uncontainable joy, energy, and enthusiasm.

Step 2: Craft a passion statement

For each passion listed, craft a statement that clearly articulates or describes that passion using fifteen words or less. An example is listed below:

To nourish the soul and awaken the spirit through food and flavor

To support this effort, ask yourself the following questions:

- What is it about this activity/experience that really excites and energizes me?
- Why am I passionate about this?

Use "the five whys" to help you. For every answer you give, keep asking yourself why until you've revealed what sits at the core of your passions, something more meaningful than because it's fun or you like it.

Step 3: Highlight your life experiences

Make a list of the pivotal moments in your life that contributed to or influenced your passions.

What you're looking for are those moments when you saw sparks or flashes of light because of the energy of the experience. You could call these your "lightning moments." This could be a time from your childhood, the first game you coached, or the first time you led a successful project, for example.

Step 4: List your strengths and core values

You've already done the hard work of identifying strengths and core values in Chapters 4 and 6.

All you have to do here is list them. This will ensure that you can easily access them for the following steps in the recipe.

Activity: The Purpose Recipe Part 2, Combine Your Ingredients
Time: 20–30 minutes

Now that you've prepared your ingredients, it's time to combine them. This is where you get to connect the dots and determine how your passions connect with your strengths and core values.

Step 1: Select a passion to focus on
You might have identified several things that you're passionate about. However, for these next steps, you'll need to focus on one passion at a time. Select one passion to focus on.

Step 2: Connect with your strengths
In the previous activity, you identified some life experiences that connect with this passion. So in this step, you're working to determine how your strengths are connected with this passion. For each of your top five strengths, describe how it enables you to live your passion.

Step 3: Align with your values
This step is all about identifying how your passion aligns with your core values. Define how your passion aligns with each of your top five values.

Daily Reinforcement: Watching for Lightning
Time: 5 minutes

This daily reinforcement is designed to help you become more aware of your passions and where they exist in your daily life.

Step 1
Take a moment and calm your thoughts by focusing on your breathing. On your inhale, say silently to yourself, "Inhale." On your exhale, say silently to yourself, "Exhale."

Don't worry if your thoughts wander a little. Just bring your thoughts back to your breath. Do this for two minutes.

Step 2
Reflect on your day and identify any moments that energized and excited you.

For example, this could be following a phone call when you helped a friend in need or when you solved a problem for your project team.

Record the following about each moment:
- Describe the moment, who was involved, and what took place
- Identify the passion this moment is connected with
- Define how this moment made you feel

Daily Reinforcement: In Service of Others
Time: 5 minutes

This daily reinforcement is designed to help you become more aware of opportunities you have to be in service of others.

Step 1

Take a moment and calm your thoughts by focusing on your breathing. On your inhale, say silently to yourself, "Inhale." On your exhale, say silently to yourself, "Exhale."

Don't worry if your thoughts wander a little. Just bring your thoughts back to your breath. Do this for two minutes.

Step 2:

Reflect on your day and ask yourself this, "How was I in service to others today?" Describe how you served others.

This could be an act of kindness, like paying for someone's coffee in the line behind you or helping your spouse prepare dinner, for example. The possibilities are endless.

 ## SWAGGER Insight

- Your purpose enables you to get back on track regardless of what life throws at you.
- Your SWAGGER can't reach its full potential without purpose.
- You already have a purpose; you just haven't uncovered it yet.
- Your purpose describes why you exist and includes an outcome that's focused on positively impacting the greater good.
- Purpose satisfies your desire for meaning and to be part of something bigger than yourself.
- Your purpose is what drives you and keeps you going even when things get tough.
- Living your purpose isn't about *you* succeeding; it's about the positive impact *you* can have on *others*.
- Purpose is the difference between merely surviving your life and thriving in it.
- When you allow your purpose to remain hidden, you're vulnerable

to the influences of external forces and more susceptible to being led down unhealthy and destructive paths.

- Uncovering your purpose isn't a nice thing to have, it's an essential component of your overall well-being and happiness.
- When you find what you're passionate about, it's as if the energy can't be contained and must find a release, similar to lightning.
- Your passions can shift and change over time.
- Your passions can lead you closer to discovering your purpose.
- Uncovering your purpose requires experimentation, analysis, and trial and error.
- Your purpose is unique to you because the ingredients used are unique to you.
- To uncover your purpose, you'll need a clear understanding of your passions, life experiences, strengths, and core values.
- Uncovering your purpose requires **P to the Power of 3 – Patience – Practice – Perseverance**.

CHAPTER 9

So, Now What?

Have you ever gotten to the end of a movie and said to yourself, "That's it? That's the end? That's where you're going to stop the story? That's the best you can do?"

Without a satisfactory conclusion, a movie like this can leave you hanging without a resolution. It's such a letdown after the build-up of the movie that you don't truly know what happens next and might feel a little at a loss.

Well, there's no fear of that here, in *Claim Your SWAGGER*, my friend, because *this isn't the end*—

This is only the beginning.

In this chapter, we'll focus on what to expect when you wholeheartedly claim your SWAGGER, why everyone isn't doing it, how to write your SWAGGER sequel, and we'll also explore steps you can take for SWAGGER success.

So, are you ready?

Well, alright then, let's do this!

From Unimaginable to Real

In the movie *Something's Gotta Give*, Diane Keaton is playwright Erica Barry. There's a scene in the movie where Erica says, "You know, I've written this, but I never really got it."

She's referring to being heartbroken, but I bring this up because what you're about to experience is unlike anything you could possibly imagine. You're about to move into a place where the unimaginable becomes real and your dreams are realized.

How do I know? Because I'm living it.

Of course, actualizing your dreams doesn't necessarily require SWAGGER. For example, I'll never forget the time I stood in the endzone of the field as a cheerleader at my first college football game. I remember thinking to myself, "Oh my goodness. This is actually happening. I made it. I'm here." I grew up watching college football games with my dad and had always dreamed of becoming a college cheerleader. My dream had become a reality, and this occurred well before I'd claimed my SWAGGER.

That being said, when you do claim your SWAGGER, you unlock your potential and increase the likelihood of accomplishing what you once thought impossible.

Imagine, for a moment, a young girl who fantasized about owning horses and the relationship she'd have with them. In these visions, her horses are her partners and her companions, not just pets. Well, I am that girl. I was born in love with horses. I had horse bedsheets, I had a miniature stable, I read horse books, and I watched movies about horses. But being in a military family made owning a horse impractical. For me, the only horses I was able to own were model ones from Breyer. All my parents kept telling me was, "I hope your husband helps choose a nice one."

As it turns out, he did, and we don't just own one, but three magnificent Arabian horses, two of which we bred ourselves. However, as described above, my dream of horses didn't merely involve owning them. No, in my dream, my horses were my partners with whom I'd have an indescribable spiritual connection and who I could confidently and competently ride.

If you recall the story I shared in Chapter 7 about my SWAGGER-limiting beliefs and my horses, you'll know that this dream was in jeopardy of being lost forever. I was so close to realizing my dream, yet the moment my instructor uttered those fateful words to me—"You'll never be able to ride your horses," I was told—it was as if it were vanishing right before my eyes.

Now, do you honestly believe I'd allow a dream I've carried my whole life to just disappear?

If you answered "no," then you'd be entirely correct. After all, I'd already claimed my SWAGGER and stepped into my power. There's absolutely no way that I was going to let someone else dictate what dreams I realized or permit my SWAGGER-limiting beliefs to get in the way of living the life I'd imagined. I'm the only one who can determine that.

Therefore, I simply made up my mind to do whatever it took to stop dreaming and start living. That meant that I needed to use the REP strategy to overcome those SWAGGER-limiting beliefs in my head and the fear they instilled. I had to spend time learning on the ground with my horses to build my confidence and earn their trust. I had to work on developing a relationship as their caregiver and leader.

So, before I was fully ready, I climbed into the saddle and began to realize my lifelong dream. I am living that dream to this day. Yes, I'm still working with my original instructor, and with another horse trainer, and none of us can believe how far I've come. The bond I've developed with my horses is more magical than anything I'd ever envisioned in my dreams.

That's the power you possess when you claim your SWAGGER. The mere fact that I'm finally realizing the dream of writing this book is a testament to the infinite possibilities that exist when you decide to tap into what makes you unique and extraordinary and when you unapologetically live your life with SWAGGER.

Perhaps you've also experienced those moments when a dream of yours is realized. Maybe it was when you graduated from college, held your child for the first time, or completed your first marathon. If so, then you know exactly what I'm talking about.

Well, now you'd better buckle up and get ready, because you're about to experience many more of these moments in your life.

When you claim your SWAGGER and practice living it, there's no end to what you can achieve and accomplish. When you're at your best, you can perform at your best and live your best life. That's what you have to look forward to. It sounds amazing, doesn't it?

It is, but it does make you wonder why more people aren't doing it.

Why Isn't Everyone Claiming Their SWAGGER?

Claiming your SWAGGER is better than any drug you'll ever take.

Granted, that's coming from someone who's never taken drugs—that's if you don't consider alcohol a drug, because I do love a fabulous glass of champagne, an expertly paired glass of wine, or an artfully crafted cocktail. Nonetheless, there's no chemical substance that can give you what your SWAGGER can. The high your SWAGGER provides doesn't fade or go away. It's always there for you. The best part is there's no letdown or hangover associated with it. How great is that?

Please recognize, I'm not saying you won't face ups and downs in your life. Of course you will; that's a given. However, your SWAGGER will be there to help you conquer whatever life puts in your path. You'll have your strengths and values to support you, your self-worth and gratitude to fortify you, and your passion and purpose to renew you. You'll have everything you need to weather the ups and downs with grace.

Right now, you're probably thinking, "Okay Jennifer, if it's so great then why isn't everyone doing it?"

Well, to that I say, "That's easy. Because it takes effort."

Claiming your SWAGGER and practicing it daily isn't like flipping a switch. You have to be willing to do the work.

Many people are looking for the "quick fix" and aren't prepared to exert themselves. They expect to lose weight and get fit by simply taking a pill, hoping that when they wake up in the morning, they'll be miraculously transformed. Or in the case of SWAGGER, that they can just read a book and the change will happen all by itself.

But oh, no, my friend, it does not work that way.

Inventor Thomas Edison said it like this: "Success is 1 percent inspiration and 99 percent perspiration."

Now you have to be prepared to put in the 99 percent. Isn't living your best life worth it?

I certainly think so.

Claiming your SWAGGER and living it daily takes faith and commitment. When you fall, you have to pick yourself back up, learn, and keep going. You have to know and believe that each setback, no matter how large or small, is strengthening your SWAGGER. You have to be able to jump, even when you don't think you're ready. You have to be willing to go against the grain and color outside the lines, even when everyone else around you is telling you that you're crazy.

For instance, my client Mira is a great example of this.

I was coaching Mira while she was getting ready to interview for a new position she'd applied for within her company. This role would be a promotion for her, and she was competing against several other people.

During our conversation, she proceeded to tell me all of the advice she'd received on how to approach the presentation she was required to give during the interview. They told her what her potential new boss was looking for, how she should structure her slides, etcetera. I could tell by the lack of energy and enthusiasm that Mira wasn't aligned with this approach.

Following additional probing and questions, Mira came up with an unorthodox idea for her presentation that would cause her to stand out from her competition. It was risky and would unquestionably require her to tap into her SWAGGER for support. However, the excitement she had for this idea was undeniable.

Mira called me the day after her presentation, and I wish I had a recording of that conversation. It was priceless. She described the moment exactly when she said, "If you're looking for someone to be a 'yes' person and agree with you, then I'm not the right fit. However, if you're looking for someone to challenge you and the way things are done, then I'm the person for the job." It was what you'd call a "drop the mic" moment.

And, yes, you guessed it, she got the job.

This is an excellent illustration of SWAGGER at work. Mira was willing to buck the system and go against what everyone told her was the best way to secure the position. She was prepared to take the risk and had trust in her SWAGGER. In the end, she pulled it off, but that took faith and commitment. She chose the road less traveled, one that not very many people would've been eager to take, and it was worth it.

Faith and commitment don't just involve coloring outside the lines, though. Sometimes it means leaping with conviction, even when you have no idea where you'll end up.

This is exactly what Jim did.

For years, Jim had been talking about doing something on his own. He had a dream of coaching and consulting others. Initially, he thought that he might begin by doing some part-time coaching while he maintained his full-time job—this was the logical and safe approach.

As time passed, however, Jim found it impossible to start something on the side with the hours his existing job demanded. Yet, the satisfaction and fulfillment he'd previously known were gone, and the nagging sensation that he'd outgrown his current role was stronger than ever. He had been in his position for over ten years, and he enjoyed the lifestyle his salary afforded. Making a change of this magnitude wasn't something that he took lightly. Nonetheless, he was convinced that it was time for him to move on and do something else that enabled him to live his passion and purpose.

Out of the blue, Jim was approached by a recruiter. He normally didn't take their calls but was intrigued by the company and role the recruiter described. This wasn't the dream he'd envisioned, but perhaps this was a stepping-stone along the way. So he agreed to meet with the company and begin the interview process.

The first interview went amazingly well, and the more he learned about the company, the more excited he became. The second interview didn't take place for several months, but when Jim walked out of it, he thought, "I nailed that! There's no way that interview could've gone any better." That feeling, along with the feedback from the recruiter, had Jim believing that this was where he was meant to be. He felt certain that he would get the job.

The final interview took place a few months later, and it went okay, but not as well as the previous two. That was when Jim began to question whether this was the path he was destined to follow or not. Then it happened. He got the call from the recruiter.

Jim didn't get the job.

You'd expect Jim to have been sad, frustrated, and upset. After all, the company had strung him along for months, and he'd become more excited with every interview.

However, he was anything but. Jim trusted in his SWAGGER and looked to his purpose for guidance. He realized that this job would've been a crutch. It would've enabled him to make a decent living and thus keep him from pursuing what he knew he was truly meant to do. He looked at this rejection as the kick in the rear he needed to take a leap, embrace his SWAGGER, and live his purpose.

In a bold move, Jim quit his job to chase his dream full time. He realized that the only way to make it a reality was to stop everything else and focus all of his time and energy on bringing it to life. Today, he runs a successful coaching and consulting practice. He's consistently attracting new corporate and private clients and is happier than he ever thought possible.

This is what it looks like to have faith and commitment. Jim had no idea whether he'd succeed or fail, yet he jumped anyway. Being firmly grounded in your SWAGGER gives you the courage to forge a path that others fear to tread.

SWAGGER isn't for everyone. It's for those willing to boldly go in the direction of their dreams and creatively overcome any obstacle in their way. Your desire to live a life with SWAGGER must be greater than the fear that keeps you from it. Your resolve must sustain you in times of uncertainty, and your tenacity must move you forward even when you can't see where the road leads.

If that's you, and you're ready, then your best self and life are waiting just around the corner. It's time to bring what you've only dared imagine to this point into focus. It's time to write your SWAGGER success story.

Your SWAGGER Sequel

It's not often that the sequel of a movie is better than the original. The reasons for this may vary. Sometimes the story gets watered down, main actors change, or a new director has a completely different vision.

I would consider this to be the exception to the rule.

Your SWAGGER sequel will be more exciting, captivating, and powerful than anything that came before it. How do I know? Because you're going to be the one who writes it and directs it. Oh, also, since you're the main character as well, there's no risk of the original cast not showing up.

See, you're the screenwriter, director, and lead actor for the movie of your life. This is your chance to craft an award-winning picture that goes down in history as one of the best films of all time. So what's the premise for this amazing story? Since this is a sequel, it takes place in the future. The things you experience and the goals you achieve as the lead character have yet to take place in reality, but you'll write them as if they've already happened.

"Wait, what?"

I get it. Right now, you might be shaking your head and rereading that last paragraph to grasp the meaning. Just stick with me here, and let's dig into the science around this, and it'll start to make more sense.

For this explanation, we turn once again to how the brain functions.

In Chapter 5, we discussed how the brain collects and categorizes information to help us make sense of the world around us. What's truly interesting about this is that the brain can't tell the difference between a memory, what's already happened, and a vision of the future. It stores and accesses all that information the same way. We also know that the brain tends to predict future events based on past experiences.

In other words, when you create a compelling vision of the future you'd like to live, your brain thinks it's already happened. That means you're more likely to make it come true. The more detailed you are with your vision, the greater the probability of success. So the more thoroughly you describe what it looks like, feels like, and smells like, the better.

As the screenwriter of this movie, your job is to bring the vision of this future to life. When and where does it take place? Who does the lead character engage with? What experiences do they have? What emotions do they exhibit when they realize a dream or accomplish a goal? Think of yourself as omniscient. You know the inner thoughts and feelings of the characters as well as when and how the events unfold.

Additionally, since you're both the screenwriter and main character of your SWAGGER sequel, you'll be writing the story in the third person. This means that you'll use your name, as well as pronouns such as "she," "he," "they," or "them" to refer to yourself. You won't use "I" or "me." This story is crafted as if you were someone sitting on the couch watching the movie of your life unfold.

For many people, myself included, talking about yourself and your accomplishments is quite difficult. By placing yourself in the role of the observer, though, you make the process a bit easier. You're no longer bragging or arrogant, you're a person on the outside looking in. That's the beauty of using third person to craft your SWAGGER sequel.

Don't get me wrong, it's still challenging when you begin. That being said, once you get out of your own way and overcome your initial reticence, the experience can be incredibly enjoyable and, dare I say, liberating.

So come on, my friend, let yourself have fun with this exercise and don't hold back.

If you're still hung up on it a little, think of it like this: writing in third person gives you license to be limitless in your creativity. You don't have to be constrained or conform to any specific rules or doctrines. You certainly don't have to craft this using a screenplay format. You can simply write it as a story. Take a look at the following example to better understand this concept.

The scene opens with Jennifer walking at her treadmill desk, which is situated in front of the windows to give her a panoramic view of the ocean. You can hear the sounds of the waves crashing in the distance.

As the camera zooms in, we see tears of joy streaming down her face. The camera focuses on what she's reading on the computer screen. The email begins with the word "Congratulations!" Her book just hit number one on the New York Times Best Sellers List.

It was a long time in the making, but she finally did it. She accomplished her dream of becoming a best-selling author.

Jennifer takes a deep breath, raises her hands in the air and screams, "Yes!"

She's overcome with emotion as she picks up the phone to share the news with her husband. All the while thinking to herself, "The champagne will be flowing tonight!" But not just yet, she has a few more calls to make first.

I could go on and on, but I think you get the idea. In this example, I can not only envision myself there, but I also know precisely what it feels like. I can physically experience the emotions the scene describes. The more imagery and emotion you can connect to your vision, the stronger the imprint is in the brain. Thus, the greater the probability is of you making the vision your new reality.

What amazing things will you achieve in your SWAGGER sequel? You might not know yet, but you're getting excited thinking about it, aren't you? Good, because you should be.

Although, it's important to remember, you can't just *write* your SWAGGER sequel, you have to *live* it.

Let's explore some steps to help you on your journey to success.

Take These Steps for SWAGGER Success

Business strategist Dan Waldschmidt had this to say about success: "The only thing standing between you and outrageous success is continuous progress."

I unreservedly agree. Every step you take moves you closer to realizing your dreams and living your best life with SWAGGER.

Nevertheless, have you ever wondered why some people seem to have an easier time achieving success than others? It's not necessarily because they worked harder than everyone else. It's more likely the result of working smarter.

That's exactly what the following steps will enable you to do, work smarter and set yourself up for SWAGGER success.

Make It Real

There's a reason why coaches and trainers have you physically write out your goals and share them publicly. It makes them real.

As we mentioned before, it's much easier to give up on yourself and a goal that no one else knows about. It's a completely different story when you've announced to the world what you aim to achieve. There's a lot more riding on your success and accomplishing what you set out to do.

The same holds true for practicing and living your SWAGGER. You have to make it real. Share your SWAGGER sequel with as many people as possible. Start small, with people who know and love you. But then, be daring and put it out there for the world to see.

To really create some accountability, you can feel free to post it on swaggeru.com/my_swagger.

I know it's a scary thought, but you've got this. You've got SWAGGER, my friend. Don't worry about the naysayers or haters that'll inevitably show up. Just remember that they're jealous of you because they're not brave enough to claim their SWAGGER on their own. They're stuck in the cheap seats, unable and unwilling to step onto the stage.

Get Support

The phrase "it takes a village" has been around for centuries. It denotes the idea that the help of many is essential to success. If you ask a successful person you know, they'll likely tell you that they didn't do it alone. Just listen to any speech given by a professional athlete following a win. They acknowledge and thank the many people on their team, including their family and friends, who helped to make it possible.

Now, think about you and your SWAGGER journey. What support structure could you put in place to help increase your chances of SWAGGER success? Who do you need on your team to succeed?

You might consider enlisting the help of a coach or mentor. Perhaps you join a community of like-minded people aimed at supporting and encouraging one another like at swaggeru.com/my_swagger. You could seek out and surround yourself with raving fans and people invested in your success.

There are many people out there who are ready and willing to support you along the way. These ideas only scratch the surface of the opportunities that exist.

You don't have to do this alone.

Practice Daily

What happens to a plant when you stop watering it?

Exactly. It withers and dies.

Your SWAGGER will do the same without day-to-day attention and care. It requires nourishment and exercise daily to not only survive but thrive. You can't expect to become adept at anything without consistent and regular practice.

Your SWAGGER isn't something you can put aside and practice every once in a while. You have to practice and live it every day. Remember to employ **P to the Power of 3 – Patience – Practice – Perseverance**. Small, doable steps lead to success. Create windows of time throughout your day for practice. You might take a break between meetings or use the time you have during your commute. You could wake up 10 minutes earlier than usual and do some practice before getting out of bed in the morning.

You get the idea.

Create a schedule that works for you, aiming for three to five practice sessions per day. Remember, your practice sessions include all aspects of working on your SWAGGER, like reviewing chapters of the book, completing corresponding activities, daily reinforcement suggestions, meeting with your coach, and connecting with the SWAGGER community on swaggeru.com/my_swagger.

Your practice doesn't have to take long, just make sure you're doing something every day to develop and support your SWAGGER. For additional activities and daily reinforcements, go to swaggeru.com/my_swagger.

Learn from Your Setbacks

There is no such thing as failure, only learning. You're bound to experience setbacks as you live your SWAGGER sequel. It's not a matter of if, but when. The most important thing to focus on is how you respond when they occur.

By accepting the fact that setbacks are a natural part of the process, you desensitize yourself to the negativity that's often associated with them. This enables you to quiet your SWAGGER-limiting beliefs so you can concentrate on learning instead. As a result, you become smarter and more capable than you were before the setback took place, and therefore, better equipped to meet what comes next.

Take the time to pause and ask yourself questions such as "What happened? What can I learn from this? What can I do differently in the future?"

The more you learn, the more you develop and grow, and the stronger your SWAGGER becomes.

Celebrate Your Successes

Your SWAGGER sequel is like a never-ending story, you'll always be writing and adding to it. You can't wait until you get to the end to celebrate. There is no end. Every step along the path helps prepare you for the next one to come. Therefore, every achievement, no matter how small, is something to be celebrated for the part it plays in moving you forward.

If this is something you struggle with, you're not alone. I'm still working on getting better at this. My natural tendency is to move to the next step without taking the time to celebrate what I've just accomplished. You can start by defining what success looks like. For example, as I was writing this book, I would use daily word counts as a small measure of success. A larger, and still interim, measure of success was when I completed a chapter. The ultimate measure of success for this part of my SWAGGER sequel was finishing the manuscript for the book.

Once success is defined, you can then determine how you'd like to celebrate. You might have a nice dinner, go for a run, have a glass of wine, or buy yourself a special treat. The possibilities are endless. The celebration could be large or small, just make sure to select something meaningful to you.

Congratulations!

Speaking of celebrating successes, what do you say we go and celebrate yours right now?

We've officially reached the conclusion of this part of your SWAGGER journey. You've been on a roller coaster ride through the SWAGGER method, and your train has finally arrived back at the station.

On this journey, you worked to develop a new relationship with your self-worth and gain an appreciation for your strengths and limitations. You learned to find gratitude for how your life experiences have shaped who you are, and you've become grounded in your core values. You became empowered to overcome your SWAGGER-limiting beliefs and were renewed by uncovering your passion and purpose.

It's been quite a ride, so congratulations on claiming your SWAGGER! I applaud your efforts and have enjoyed every minute you've allowed me to spend with you along the way. It's been my distinct honor and privilege to share the SWAGGER method with you.

As I said at the start of this chapter, this isn't the end; it's only the beginning. Your SWAGGER sequel is a never-ending story that you'll be forever crafting. It's definitely a movie I can't wait to see.

In the meantime, do me a favor, go and live your SWAGGER unapologetically. Also, you can always find me at swaggeru.com if you need additional help and guidance, and until we meet again, just remember that you've got this!

ABOUT THE AUTHOR

Jennifer **Mrozek Sukalo** is a transformational expert, performance coach,
and the creator of SWAGGER U, a
personal development approach to harnessing
your untapped potential and becoming who
you were born to be. Jennifer has focused her
career on helping people, as a global leadership
consultant, transformational coach, and fitness professional. She spent the past ten years
helping high-performing individuals at vari-
ous multinational Fortune 500 companies create positive and sustainable
change in themselves to become better for those they lead. Her work in
leadership development and coaching cancer survivors to transform their
circumstances from "survival" to a "spark for the rest of their lives" laid the
groundwork for the SWAGGER method.

A passionate home chef, curious traveler, and avid fly-fisher, Jennifer lives
in New Canaan, Connecticut, with her husband. Her three Arabian horses,
Tana, Rocco, and Tank keep her humble and grounded.

REFERENCES

Adolphs, Ralph, and David J Anderson. 2018. *The Neuroscience of Emotion: A New Synthesis*. Princeton and Oxford: Princeton University Press.

Baars, Bernard J., and Nicole M Gage. 2010. Cognition, Brain, and Consciousness: Introduction to Cognitive Neuroscience, Second Edition. Academic Press.

Beck, Martha. 2001. Finding Your Own North Star: Claiming the Life You Were Meant to Live. New York: Three Rivers Press.

Biello, David. 2007. "Back to the Future: How the Brain 'Sees' the Future." *Scientific American*, January 2. https://www.scientificamerican.com/article/back-to-the-future-how-th/.

Brown, Brené. 2018. *Dare to Lead: Brave Work. Tough Conversations. Whole Hearts*. New York: Random House.

Celestine, Nicole. 2015. "How to Change Self-Limiting Beliefs According to Psychology." *Positive Psychology*, November 24. https://positivepsychology.com/false-beliefs/.

Chamine, Shirzad. 2012. *Positive Intelligence: Why Only 20% of Teams and Individuals Achieve Their True Potential and How You Can Achieve Yours*. Austin, Tx: Greenleaf Book Group Press.

Cherry, Kendra. 2022. "5 Reasons Emotions are Important." *Very Well Mind*, July 22. https://www.verywellmind.com/the-purpose-of-emotions-2795181.

Climer, Amy. 2017. "How Experiences Shape Our Lives." *Climer Consulting* (blog). https://climerconsulting.com/experiences-shape-lives/.

Dweck, Carol S. 2008. *Mindset: The New Psychology of Success*. New York: Ballantine Books.

Gleeson, Brent. 2021. "Why Core Values Matter (and How to get Your Team Excited About Them)." *Forbes*, March 30. https://www.forbes.com/sites/brentgleeson/2021/03/30/why-core-values-matter-and-how-to-get-your-team-excited-about-them/?sh=29242ea04afd.

Ibarra, Herminia. 2015. "The Authenticity Paradox." *Harvard Business Review*, January-February. https://hbr.org/2015/01/the-authenticity-paradox.

Ikigai Living. 2022. "Ikigai: The Japanese Answer to a Life of Purpose: A Comprehensive Look into the True Meaning of Ikigai." https://ikigai-living.com/what-is-ikigai/.

Kirova, Daniela. 2021. "What are Core Values and Why are They Important." Values Institute, February 23. https://values.institute/what-are-core-values-and-why-are-they-important/.

Lally, Phillipa, Cornelia H.M. Van Jaarsveld, Henry W.W. Potts, and Jane Wardle. 2009. "How Are Habits Formed: Modelling Habit Formation in the Real World." *European Journal of Social Psychology*, July 16. https://onlinelibrary.wiley.com/doi/10.1002/ejsp.674.

Lipton, Bruce H. 2005. *The Biology of Belief: Unleashing the Power of Consciousness, Matter & Miracles*. Hay House, Inc.

Mercurio, Zach. 2017. *The Invisible Leader: Transform Your Life, Work, and Organizations with the Power of Authentic Purpose*. Charleston, SC: Advantage.

Miller, Hannah L., 2022. "Self-Limiting Beliefs: A Guide for Overcoming Limitations." *Leaders*, June 3. https://leaders.com/articles/personal-growth/limiting-beliefs/.

Pennebaker, James W., and John F Evans. 2014. *Expressive Writing: Words that Heal*. Enumclaw, WA: Idyll Arbor, Incorporated.

Pink, Daniel H. 2009. *Drive: The Surprising Truth About What Motivates Us*. New York: Riverhead Books.

Quora. 2018. "How Emotions Shape the Way We Experience the World." *Forbes*, January 4. https://www.forbes.com/sites/quora/2018/01/04/how-emotions-shape-the-way-we-experience-the-world/?sh=482b47864782.

Schacter, Daniel L., Donna Rose Addis, Demis Hassabis, Victoria C. Martin, R. Nathan Spreng, and Karl K. Szpunar. 2012. "The Future of

Memory: Remembering, Imagining, and the Brain." *Neuron* (November 21): doi: 10.1016/j.neuron.2012.11.001.

Seligman, Martin E. P. 2006. *Learned Optimism: How to Change Your Mind and Your Life*. New York: Vintage Books.

Sinek, Simon. 2009. *Start with Why: How Great Leaders Inspire Everyone to Take Action*. Penguin Group.

Swart, Tara, Kitty Chisholm, and Paul Brown. 2015. *Neuroscience for Leadership: Harnessing the Brain Gain Advantage*. England: Palgrave Macmillan.

Wizeman, Liz, with Greg McKeown. 2010 *Multipliers: How the Best Leaders Make Everyone Smarter*. Harper Collins.

A free ebook edition is available with the purchase of this book.

To claim your free ebook edition:

1. Visit MorganJamesBOGO.com
2. Sign your name CLEARLY in the space
3. Complete the form and submit a photo of the entire copyright page
4. You or your friend can download the ebook to your preferred device

Morgan James BOGO™

A **FREE** ebook edition is available for you or a friend with the purchase of this print book.

CLEARLY SIGN YOUR NAME ABOVE

Instructions to claim your free ebook edition:
1. Visit MorganJamesBOGO.com
2. Sign your name CLEARLY in the space above
3. Complete the form and submit a photo of this entire page
4. You or your friend can download the ebook to your preferred device

Print & Digital Together Forever.

Snap a photo

Free ebook

Read anywhere